THE ROMAN RITUAL

Revised by decree
of the Second Vatican Ecumenical Council
and published by authority of Pope Paul VI

RITE
OF
RELIGIOUS
PROFESSION

D1601697

Prepared by
International Commission on English in the Liturgy
A Joint Commission of Catholic Bishops' Conferences
and
Secretariat for the Liturgy
National Conference of Catholic Bishops

1989

Concordat cum originali: Reverend Ronald F. Krisman
Executive Director
Secretariat for the Liturgy
National Conference of Catholic Bishops

ISBN 1-55586-273-X

CONTENTS

FOREWORD

On February 2, 1970, the Congregation for Divine Worship issued the Latin typical edition of *Ordo professionis religiosae.* An interim English translation was prepared by the International Commission on English in the Liturgy (ICEL) in 1971. A second revised edition was issued by ICEL in 1974.

On September 12, 1983, the Congregation for the Sacraments and Divine Worship published *Emendations in the Liturgical Books following upon the New Code of Canon Law.* This document indicates all the changes that are to be made in the liturgical books as a result of the promulgation of the revised *Code of Canon Law* of 1983. The most notable change made in the *Rite of Religious Profession* to conform it to the new *Code of Canon Law* is the deletion of the Rite of a Promise and of all references to it in the Introduction.

This revised edition of *The Rite of Religious Profession* contains all the changes mandated by the *Emendations,* as well as the 1982 revised translation of the Introduction to the rite, taken from *Documents on the Liturgy, 1963-1979: Conciliar, Papal, and Curial Texts.* In addition, the publication of this new edition has been the occasion for making several corrections in the text of the previous edition.

Secretariat for the Liturgy
National Conference
of Catholic Bishops

1

SACRED CONGREGATION
FOR DIVINE WORSHIP

Prot. n. 200/70

DECREE

The rite of profession by which religious, in commitment to the evangelical counsels, vow themselves to God, has been revised in accord with the intent of the *Constitution on the Liturgy*. The life dedicated to God by the bonds of religious life has always held a place of high honor in the eyes of the Church, which from the earliest centuries has surrounded the act of religious profession with liturgical rites. The Fathers of Vatican Council II directed that a rite of religious profession and renewal of vows be drawn up that would contribute to greater unity, simplicity, and dignity and that, apart from exceptions in particular law, it should be adopted by those who make their profession of renewal of vows within Mass (art. 80).

Carrying out this directive, the Consilium has composed the present rite of religious profession; Pope Paul VI by his apostolic authority has approved it and ordered that it be incorporated into the *Roman Ritual* and published. Consequently this Congregation for Divine Worship, at the explicit mandate of the Pope, promulgates this rite.

The conferences of bishops (where applicable, through the joint commission of nations of the same language) are to see to the careful vernacular translations of the rite, after consultation with the conferences of major religious superiors in each country.

The rite of profession must be an expression of the identity and spirit of the individual religious family. Therefore each religious institute should adapt this rite in such a way that the ritual clearly brings out the institute's special character, then send the rite to this Congregation as soon as possible for confirmation.

All things to the contrary notwithstanding.

From the Sacred Congregation for Divine Worship, 2 February 1970, the feast of the Presentation of the Lord.

+ Benno Cardinal Gut
Prefect

A. Bugnini
Secretary

INTRODUCTION*

I. NATURE AND IMPORT
OF RELIGIOUS PROFESSION

1. In response to God's call many Christians dedicate themselves to his service and to the welfare of humanity through the sacred bonds of religious life and seek to follow Christ more closely through the evangelical counsels.[1] This leads to the grace of baptism achieving richer results in them.[2]

2. The Church has always esteemed the religious life, which, under the guidance of the Holy Spirit, has taken various forms in the course of history.[3] It has raised religious life to the rank of a canonical state and approved a great number of religious institutes and protected them by wise legislation.[4]

For it is the Church that receives the vows of those who make religious profession, begs God's grace for them by its public prayer, puts them in God's hands, blesses them, and unites their offering with the eucharistic sacrifice.[5]

---

* The text here is based on the second printing, which carries the following note: "It is necessary to reprint the *Order professionis religiosae*, first published in 1970." Therefore it seemed advisable to provide this reprint with certain minor changes:

1. The texts of the psalms and of the New Testament have been taken from the Neo-Vulgate edition of the Bible.

2. There are some emendations of titles and rubrics in order that these might more clearly respond to the language and style found in the liturgical books published since 1969.

3. The liturgical texts can be adapted to fit particular situations by a change in gender or number.

II. RITES FOR THE DIFFERENT STAGES OF RELIGIOUS LIFE

3. The steps by which religious dedicate themselves to God and the Church are these: novitiate, first profession (or other sacred bonds), and

final profession. The constitutions of religious institutes add to these a renewal of vows.

4. The novitiate, the beginning of life in the institute,[6] is a time of testing for both novice and community. Entry into the novitiate should be marked by a rite in which God's grace is sought for the special purpose of the period. This rite should, of its nature, be restrained and simple, celebrated in the presence only of the religious community. It should take place outside Mass.

5. First profession then follows. Through temporary vows before God and the Church the novices promise to observe the evangelical counsels. Such vows may be taken within Mass, but without special solemnity. The rite of first profession provides for the bestowal of insignia of the religious life and the habit, following the very ancient custom of giving the habit at the end of the period of probation, since the habit is a sign of consecration.[7]

6. After the period prescribed by law, final profession is made, by which religious bind themselves permanently to the service of God and the Church. Perpetual profession reflects the unbreakable union between Christ and his Bride, the Church.[8]

It is very fitting that the rite of final profession should take place within Mass, with due solemnity and in the presence of the religious community and the people.[9] The rite consists of these parts:

a. the calling or asking of those to be professed (this may be omitted if desired);

b. the homily or address, which reminds the people and those to be professed of the value of religious life;

c. the examination, by which the celebrant or superior asks those who are to be professed whether they are prepared to be consecrated to God and to follow the way of perfect charity, according to the rule of their religious family;

d. the litanies, in which prayer is offered to God the Father and the intercession of the Blessed Virgin Mary and all the saints is invoked;

e. the profession, made in the presence of the Church, the lawful superior of the institute, the witnesses, and the congregation;

f. the solemn blessing or consecration of the professed, by which the Church ratifies their profession through a liturgical consecration, asking the heavenly Father to pour forth upon them the gifts of the Holy Spirit;

g. the presentation of the insignia of profession, if this is the custom of the religious family, as outward signs of perpetual dedication to God.

7. In some religious communities vows are renewed at fixed times in accordance with the constitutions.

This renewal of vows may take place within Mass, but without solemnity, especially if renewal of vows is frequent or annual.

A liturgical rite has place only in the case of renewal of vows that has the force of law. In many religious communities, however, the custom of renewing vows has become established as an exercise of devotion. It may be carried out in many ways; but the practice of doing publicly within Mass what belongs to private devotion is not to be encouraged. If it seems appropriate to renew vows publicly on special anniversaries, for example, the twenty-fifth or fiftieth year of religious life, the rite for the renewal of vows may be used with the necessary adaptations.

8. Since all these rites have their own special character, each demands a celebration of its own. The celebration of several rites within the same liturgical service is to be absolutely excluded.

III. MASS FOR THE RITE OF RELIGIOUS PROFESSION

9. Whenever religious profession, and especially final profession, takes place within Mass, it is appropriate to choose one of the ritual Masses for the day of religious profession from the *Roman Missal* or from approved propers. In the case of a Sunday of Advent, Lent or Easter, of any solemnity, or of Ash Wednesday and all of Holy Week, the Mass is that of the day; but the special formularies for the professed during the eucharistic prayer and the final blessing may be retained.

10. Since the liturgy of the word for the rite of profession can be an important aid to bringing out the meaning of religious life and its responsibilities, it is lawful, when the Mass for the day of religious profession may not be used, to take one reading from the special list of readings for the rite of profession. But this may not be done during the Easter triduum, on the solemnities of Christmas, Epiphany, Ascension, Pentecost or Corpus Christi, or on other solemnities of obligation.

11. White vestments are worn for the ritual Mass for the day of religious profession.

IV. ADAPTATIONS TO BE MADE BY INDIVIDUAL INSTITUTES

12. The norms governing the rite of initiation (nos. 1-13 of the ritual) are not of obligation unless this is clearly stated (as in the prohibition of having the rite within Mass, no. 2) or the nature of the rite so demands (as in the rule that the rite should be restrained and simple, no. 3).

13. All who make or renew their religious profession within Mass must use the rites of temporary profession, final profession, or renewal of vows, unless they possess a particular right in this matter.[10]

14. Religious families should adapt the rite so that it more closely reflects and manifests the character and spirit of each institute. For this purpose the faculty of adapting the rite is given to each institute; its decisions are then to be reviewed by the Apostolic See.

In making adaptations in the rite of profession, the following points should be especially respected:

a. The rite takes place immediately after the gospel.

b. The arrangement of parts must remain intact, but some parts may be omitted or others of a similar nature substituted.

c. A liturgical distinction between perpetual profession and temporary profession or renewal of vows must be strictly maintained. What is proper to one rite may not be inserted into another.

d. As is stated in the pertinent places, many formularies in the rite of profession may be changed, and in fact must be, to reflect more clearly the character and spirit of each institute. Where the Roman

Ritual offers several optional formularies, particular rituals may add others of the same kind.

15. Profession in the presence of the blessed sacrament, prior to communion, is not in harmony with a true understanding of the liturgy. Henceforth, then, new religious communities are forbidden to adopt the practice. Institutes that follow this practice on the basis of a particular law are urged to discontinue it.

Similarly, all religious following a rite proper to them are instructed to embrace and follow authentic liturgical forms, putting aside anything in conflict with the principles of the liturgical reform. This is the way to achieve that simplicity, dignity, and closer unity that the Council has so strongly endorsed.[11]

NOTES

[1] See *Lumen Gentium*, "Dogmatic Constitution on the Church" (hereafter = LG), no. 43; *Perfectae Caritatis*, "Decree on the Appropriate Renewal of Religious Life" (hereafter = PC), no. 1.

[2] See LG, no. 43.

[3] See LG, no. 43; PC, no. 1.

[4] See LG, no. 45; PC, no. 1.

[5] See LG, no. 45.

[6] See *Codex Iuris Canonici*, "Code of Canon Law" (hereafter = CIC), c. 646.

[7] See PC, no. 17.

[8] See LG, no. 44.

[9] See *Sacrosanctum Concilium*, "Constitution on the Sacred Liturgy" (hereafter = SC), art. 80.

[10] See SC, art. 80.

[11] See ibid.

PART I

RITE
OF
RELIGIOUS
PROFESSION
FOR MEN

Chapter I

NORMS FOR
THE RITE OF INITIATION
INTO THE RELIGIOUS LIFE

1. *On the day when the canonical novitiate begins, it is fitting that there should be a ceremony to ask God's grace for achieving the special purpose of the novitiate.*

2. *It is forbidden to perform the rite of initiation during Mass.*

3. *The rite is to be very simple and direct, in the presence of the religious community only.*

4. *The texts for the rite must avoid anything that may seem to diminish the novices' freedom of choice or obscure the true meaning of a noviceship or time of testing.*

5. *The chapter hall or other similar room is an appropriate setting for the rite. If it seems necessary, however, the rite may take place in the chapel.*

OUTLINE OF THE RITE

INTRODUCTORY RITES

Greeting or Song
Questioning of the Postulants
 or Request for Admission
Opening Prayer

CELEBRATION OF THE WORD OF GOD

CONCLUDING RITES

General Intercessions
Lord's Prayer
Concluding Prayer

RITE OF INITIATION
INTO THE RELIGIOUS LIFE

It is appropriate that the rite should take place during a special celebration of the word on the nature of the religious life and the spirit of the institute.

INTRODUCTORY RITES

GREETING OR SONG

6. *The rite may appropriately begin with a greeting by the superior, or the singing of a psalm or other suitable hymn.*

QUESTIONING OF THE POSTULANTS
OR REQUEST FOR ADMISSION

7. *Then the superior questions the postulants in these or similar words:*

Dear sons (brothers), what do you ask from us?

The postulants reply together in these or similar words:

We wish to try your way of life,
and are willing to be tested ourselves,
that we may follow Christ wholeheartedly
in this community of N.

The superior replies:

May the Lord grant you his help.
R. Amen.

Drawn by God's mercy,
we have come here to learn your way of life.
We ask you to teach us to follow Christ crucified
and to live in poverty, obedience and chastity.
Teach us to persevere in prayer and penance,
in the service of the Church and of humankind.
Teach us to be one with you in heart and mind.
Help us to live out the Gospel every day of our lives.
Teach us your rule and help us to learn to love
our brothers as Christ commanded us.

Or he may use similar words, expressing the aspirations and thoughts of the postulants themselves.

The superior responds in these or similar words:

May God in his mercy be with you always
and may Christ our teacher grant light to us all.

R. Amen.

OPENING PRAYER

9. *After the questioning or request for admission, the superior says:*

Let us pray.

Lord God,
you give us the desire to hear your call.
Listen favorably to the prayers of your servants N. and N.,
who, desiring to serve you more perfectly,
ask to join our community.
Grant that our life in common
may become a communion of love.

We ask this through Christ our Lord.

R. Amen.

CELEBRATION OF THE WORD OF GOD

10. *Suitable texts from holy Scripture are then read, with appropriate responsories (see nos. 91-136).*

11. *At their conclusion the superior addresses the religious community and the postulants on the meaning of the religious life and the spirit of the institute, or he reads an appropriate chapter of the rule.*

CONCLUDING RITES

12. *The rite fittingly concludes with the general intercessions (prayer of the faithful) and the Lord's Prayer, to which a suitable prayer may be added, such as:*

Lord God,
you call us to your service
and inspire us to hear your call.
These brothers of ours
desire to test our way of life:
help them to know what you ask of them
and strengthen us all in your service.

We ask this through Christ our Lord.

R. Amen.

13. *After this the superior entrusts the newly admitted novices to the care of the novice master, and with his fellow religious greets them in the spirit of Christian love in the way customary in the religious community. Meanwhile, an appropriate song or canticle of praise is sung.*

Chapter II

RITE OF
TEMPORARY PROFESSION
DURING MASS

---

14. *The rite described in this chapter takes place during Mass. It may be used only for those religious who make their first profession upon successful completion of the novitiate (see Introduction, no. 5).*

15. *The Mass may correspond to the liturgy of the day, or the ritual Mass for the day of first profession may be used, in accordance with the rubrics (see Introduction, nos. 9-11).*

16. *In clerical institutes it is proper for the superior who receives the profession to preside over the eucharistic sacrifice. In lay institutes a chair should be prepared in a convenient part of the sanctuary for the superior who is to receive the profession of the members of the institute.*

17. *The profession ordinarily takes place at the chair; if circumstances so dictate, the chair may be placed in front of the altar. Seats should be so arranged in the sanctuary for those making profession that the faithful have a complete view of the liturgical rites.*

18. *Enough bread and wine for consecration should be prepared for the ministers, those making their profession, and their parents, relatives, and fellow religious. If only one chalice is used, it should be sufficiently large.*

19. *In addition to what is needed for Mass, there should also be ready:*

   a) the ritual for religious profession;
   b) the religious habit, if the religious institute has decided to present it on the occasion of first profession (see Introduction, no. 5);
   c) the book of the rule or constitutions, and other insignia of religious profession which, according to law or custom, are to be presented.

OUTLINE OF THE RITE

INTRODUCTORY RITES

LITURGY OF THE WORD

RELIGIOUS PROFESSION
Calling or Request
Homily or Address
Examination
Prayer for God's Grace
Profession
Presentation of the Insignia
  of Religious Profession
    Presentation of the Religious Habit
    Presentation of the Rule or Constitutions
General Intercessions

LITURGY OF THE EUCHARIST

RITE OF TEMPORARY PROFESSION DURING MASS

INTRODUCTORY RITES

20. *When the people and the religious are assembled and everything is ready, the procession moves through the church to the altar in the usual way, while the choir and people sing the entrance song of the Mass. Those to be professed may fittingly join in the procession, accompanied by the novice master and, in lay institutes, the superior.*

21. *When they come to the sanctuary all make the customary reverence to the altar and go to their places; then Mass continues.*

LITURGY OF THE WORD

22. *The liturgy of the word takes place as usual, except for the following:*

a) the readings may be taken from the Mass of the day or from the texts in nos. 91-136 (see Introduction, nos. 9-10);

b) the profession of faith may be omitted, even if prescribed by the rubrics of the day.

RELIGIOUS PROFESSION

CALLING OR REQUEST

23. After the gospel the celebrant and the people sit, but those to be professed stand. Then, according to choice or as circumstances demand, the deacon or the novice master calls those to be professed by name.

They answer:

Present,

or they make some other reply according to local usage or the custom of the religious community.

24. The celebrant then questions them in these or similar words:

My dear brothers (sons), what do you ask of God and of his holy Church?

The candidates reply together in these or similar words:

We ask for God's merciful love
and for the grace of serving him more perfectly
in your (this) religious community.

The celebrant and all the members of the religious community reply:

Thanks be to God,

or they express their approval in some other way.

---

25. The calling by name and the questioning by the celebrant may be omitted; a request by those to be professed may take their place. For example, one of those to be professed may stand facing the celebrant (or superior) and say, in the name of all, these or similar words:

With the help of God,
we (N. and N.) have studied your rule
and have lived among you as your brothers for the time
of probation.

Father (Brother), we now ask to be allowed
to dedicate ourselves to God and his kingdom
by making profession in this religious community of N.

The celebrant and all the members of the religious community reply:

Thanks be to God,

or they express their approval in some other way.

HOMILY OR ADDRESS

26. *Those to be professed then sit and listen to the homily or address which should develop the scriptural readings and the theme of religious profession as God's gift and call for the sanctification of those chosen and for the good of the Church and the whole human family.*

EXAMINATION

27. *After the homily or address, those to be professed stand, and the celebrant questions them on their readiness to dedicate themselves to God and to seek perfect charity, according to the rule or constitutions of the religious community. The questions may be changed or in part omitted, to suit the spirit and character of each religious institute.*

The celebrant questions them, saying:

My dear sons (brothers),
by water and the Holy Spirit
you have already been consecrated to God's service:
are you resolved to unite yourselves more closely to him
by the new bond of religious profession?

They answer:

I am.

The celebrant continues:

In your desire to follow Christ perfectly,
are you resolved to live in chastity
for the sake of the kingdom of heaven,
to choose a life of poverty,
and to offer the sacrifice of obedience?

They answer:

I am.

28. *Then the celebrant confirms their intention in these or similar words:*

May almighty God grant you his grace
to fulfill what you resolve.

R. Amen.

PRAYER FOR GOD'S GRACE

29. *The celebrant then prays for God's help, saying:*

Let us pray.

All pray for a while in silence. Then the celebrant says:

Lord,
look upon these servants of yours
who are resolved to dedicate their lives to you
by making profession of the evangelical counsels
in the presence of your Church today.
Mercifully grant that their manner of life
may bring glory to your name
and further your loving plan of redemption.

We ask this through Christ our Lord.

R. Amen.

PROFESSION

30. *After the prayer, if it is the custom of the religious community, two professed religious stand near the celebrant (or superior) to act as witnesses. Those to be professed come, one by one, to the celebrant (or superior) and read the formula of profession.*

If there are very many religious making their profession, the formula of profession may be recited by all together. The concluding words, This I promise . . . *or the like, must be said by each individually as a clear expression of his will. Then they return to their places and remain standing.*

PRESENTATION OF THE INSIGNIA OF RELIGIOUS PROFESSION

PRESENTATION OF THE RELIGIOUS HABIT

31. *After this the novice master and some members of the community present the religious habit to each of the newly professed to put on in the sanctuary or other suitable place. Meanwhile the choir may begin the antiphon:*

Lord, these are the men who long to see your face,
who seek the face of the God of Jacob (Psalm 24:6),

with Psalm 24; or some other appropriate song may be sung. The antiphon is repeated after every two verses; at the end of the psalm Glory to the Father *is not said but only the antiphon. If the presentation of the habits comes to an end before the whole psalm is sung, the psalm is interrupted and the antiphon repeated.*

PRESENTATION OF THE RULE OR CONSTITUTIONS

32. *Then, if customary, the newly professed, wearing the religious habit, come to the celebrant (or superior) who gives each the book of the rule or constitutions, saying these or similar words:*

Receive the rule of our (this) religious community.
By keeping it faithfully, may you arrive at the perfection of love.

The professed replies:

Amen.

After receiving the book, he returns to his place and remains standing.

33. *If the newly professed are numerous or there is some other reason, the celebrant (or superior) may present the rule and say the formula once only in these or similar words:*

Receive the rule of our (this) religious community.
By keeping it faithfully, may you arrive at the perfection of love.

The professed reply together:

Amen.

Then they come forward to the celebrant (superior) who gives each the book of the rule or constitutions. After receiving the book, they return to their places and remain standing.

34. *If, in accordance with the rules or customs of the religious community, other insignia of religious profession are to be presented, this is done now in silence or with a suitable formula. In this matter a dignified simplicity should be observed.*

35. *An alternative way of presenting the insignia of profession is described in nos. 137-139.*

GENERAL INTERCESSIONS

36. *The rite fittingly concludes with the general intercessions (prayer of the faithful). For these, the formula given in nos. 140-142 may be used.*

LITURGY OF THE EUCHARIST

37. *During the offertory song, some of the newly professed religious may bring the bread, wine, and water to the altar for the eucharistic sacrifice.*

38. *If it seems opportune, the celebrant gives the sign of peace to each of the newly professed religious in the usual way or in accordance with the customs of the religious community or of the place.*

39. *After the celebrant has received the body and blood of Christ, the newly professed religious come to the altar to receive communion, which may be given to them under both kinds. Then their parents, relatives, and fellow religious may receive communion in the same way.*

Chapter III

RITE OF
PERPETUAL PROFESSION
DURING MASS

---

40. *It is fitting that the rite of profession by which a religious binds himself to God for ever should take place on a Sunday or a solemnity of the Lord, of the Blessed Virgin Mary, or of a saint distinguished in the living of the religious life.*

41. *The rite of perpetual profession takes place separately from other rites of profession (see Introduction, no. 8).*

42. *Notice of the day and hour should be given to the faithful in good time so that they may attend in greater numbers.*

43. *The Mass is that of the liturgy of the day, or the ritual Mass for the day of perpetual profession may be used, in accordance with the rubrics (see Introduction, nos. 9-11).*

44. *Where possible and if the needs of the faithful do not demand individual celebration by the priests present, it is preferable that the Mass be concelebrated. If the superior who is to receive the profession is a priest, he should be the celebrant.*

45. *Profession ordinarily takes place in the church of the religious community. For pastoral reasons, however, or in order to promote esteem for the religious life, to give edification to the people of God, or to permit larger attendance, the rite may take place in the cathedral, parish church, or some other notable church, as may seem fitting.*

46. *Similarly, where religious from two or more institutes wish to celebrate their profession at the same eucharistic sacrifice, the rite of profession may suitably take place in the cathedral, a parish church, or some other notable church with the bishop presiding and the superiors of the institutes concelebrating. Those making their profession will pronounce their vows before their respective superiors.*

47. *As the nature of the rite demands, the whole liturgical service should be celebrated with fitting solemnity, but any appearance of lavishness unbecoming to religious poverty should be avoided.*

48. *The profession ordinarily takes place at the chair. To enable the faithful to take part more easily, the celebrant's chair may be placed in front of the altar. In lay institutes, a chair is to be prepared in a suitable part of the sanctuary for the superior who is to receive the profession of the members of the institute. Seats should be so arranged in the sanctuary for those making profession that the faithful may have a complete view of the liturgical rites.*

49. *Enough bread and wine for consecration should be prepared for the ministers, those making their profession, and their parents, relatives, and fellow religious. If only one chalice is used, it should be sufficiently large.*

50. *In addition to what is needed for Mass, there should also be ready:*

a) the ritual for religious profession;
b) the insignia of religious profession, if these are to be presented in accordance with the rules or customs of the religious community.

OUTLINE OF THE RITE

INTRODUCTORY RITES

LITURGY OF THE WORD

RELIGIOUS PROFESSION
Calling or Request
Homily or Address
Examination
Litany
Profession
Solemn Blessing or Consecration
  of the Professed
Presentation of the Insignia of Profession
Statement of Admission or Sign of Peace

LITURGY OF THE EUCHARIST

CONCLUDING RITE
Solemn Blessing

RITE OF PERPETUAL PROFESSION DURING MASS

INTRODUCTORY RITES

51. *When the people and the religious are assembled and everything is ready, the procession moves through the church to the altar in the usual way, while the choir and people sing the entrance song of the Mass. Those to be professed may fittingly join in the procession, accompanied by the novice master and, in lay institutes, the superior. When they come to the sanctuary, all make the customary reverence to the altar and go to their places; then Mass continues.*

LITURGY OF THE WORD

52. *The liturgy of the word takes place as usual, except for the following:*

   a) the readings may be taken from the Mass of the day or from the texts in nos. 91-136 (see Introduction, nos. 9-10);

   b) the profession of faith may be omitted, even if prescribed by the rubrics of the day;

   c) the general intercessions in the form customarily used during the celebration of Mass are omitted (see no. 62).

RELIGIOUS PROFESSION

CALLING OR REQUEST

53. After the gospel the celebrant and the people sit, but those to be professed stand. Then, according to choice or as circumstances demand, the deacon or the novice master calls those to be professed by name.

They answer:

Present,

or they make some other reply according to local usage or the custom of the religious community.

54. The celebrant then questions them in these or similar words:

My dear brothers (sons), what do you ask of God and of his holy Church?

The candidates reply together in these or similar words:

We ask for perseverance in God's service
and in your (this) religious community
all the days of our lives.

The celebrant and all the members of the religious community reply:

Thanks be to God,

or they express their approval in some other way.

---

55. The calling by name and the questioning by the celebrant may be omitted; a request by those to be professed may take their place. For example, one of those to be professed may stand facing the celebrant (or superior) and say, in the name of all, these or similar words:

With the help of God,
we (N. and N.) have come to know
the life of religious dedication in your community.

Father (Brother), we now ask to be allowed
to make perpetual profession in this religious community of N.
for the glory of God and the service of the Church.

*The celebrant and all the members of the religious community
reply:*

Thanks be to God,

or they express their approval in some other way.

HOMILY OR ADDRESS

56. *Those to be professed then sit and listen to the homily or address which should develop the scriptural readings and the theme
of religious profession as God's gift and call for the sanctification
of those chosen and for the good of the Church and the whole
human family.*

EXAMINATION

57. *After the homily or address, those to be professed stand, and
the celebrant questions them on their readiness to dedicate themselves to God and to seek perfect charity, according to the rule or
constitutions of the religious community. The questions may be
changed or in part omitted, to suit the spirit and character of
each religious institute.*

The celebrant questions them, saying:

Dear sons (brothers),
in baptism you have already died to sin
and been consecrated to God's service.
Are you now resolved to unite yourself more closely to God
by the bond of perpetual profession?

They answer:

I am.

The celebrant continues:

Are you resolved,
with the help of God,
to undertake that life of perfect chastity, obedience, and poverty
chosen for themselves by Christ our Lord and his Virgin Mother,
and to persevere in it for ever?

They answer:

I am.

The celebrant continues:

Are you resolved to strive steadfastly for perfection
in the love of God and of your neighbor
by living the Gospel with all your heart
and keeping the rule of this religious community?

They answer:

I am.

The celebrant continues:

Are you resolved,
with the help of the Holy Spirit,
to spend your whole life in the generous service of God's people?

They answer:

I am.

58. *In the case of religious communities wholly dedicated to the contemplative life, this may appropriately be added:*

The celebrant asks:

Are you resolved to live for God alone,
in solitude and silence,
in persevering prayer and willing penance,
in humble work and holiness of life?

They answer:

I am.

59. *At the end of the questions, the celebrant confirms the intention of those to be professed in these or similar words:*

May God who has begun the good work in you
bring it to fulfillment
before the day of Christ Jesus.

All:

Amen.

LITANY

60. *All then rise. The celebrant stands, with hands joined, and says, facing the people:*

Dear friends in Christ,
let us pray to God the almighty Father
for these servants of his
whom he has called to follow Christ in the religious life;
in his love may he bless them with his grace
and strengthen them in their holy purpose.

61. *The deacon gives the sign to kneel.*

Let us kneel.

The celebrant kneels at his chair. Those to be professed prostrate themselves or kneel, according to the custom of the place or of the religious community. The rest kneel. During the Easter Season and on all Sundays, all stand except those to be professed.

62. *Then the cantors sing the litany for the rite of religious profession, all making the responses. In this litany one or the other of the petitions marked with the same letter may be omitted. At the appropriate place there may be inserted invocations of saints especially venerated in the religious community or by the faithful; other petitions may be added to suit the occasion.*

Lord, have mercy
Christ, have mercy
Lord, have mercy

Lord, have mercy
Christ, have mercy
Lord, have mercy

Holy Mary, Mother of God	pray for us
Saint Michael	pray for us
Holy angels of God	pray for us
Saint John the Baptist	pray for us
Saint Joseph	pray for us
Saint Peter and Saint Paul	pray for us
Saint John	pray for us
Saint Mary Magdalene	pray for us
Saint Stephen and Saint Lawrence	pray for us
Saint Agnes	pray for us
Saint Basil	pray for us
Saint Augustine	pray for us
Saint Benedict	pray for us
Saint Bernard	pray for us
Saint Francis and Saint Dominic	pray for us
Saint Ignatius of Loyola	pray for us
Saint Vincent de Paul	pray for us
Saint John Bosco	pray for us
Saint Catherine of Siena	pray for us
Saint Teresa of Jesus	pray for us
All holy men and women	pray for us
Lord, be merciful	Lord, save your people
From all evil	Lord, save your people
From every sin	Lord, save your people
From everlasting death	Lord, save your people
By your coming as man	Lord, save your people
By your death and rising to new life	Lord, save your people
By your gift of the Holy Spirit	Lord, save your people
Be merciful to us sinners	Lord, hear our prayer

a) By the self-offering of your servants
and their apostolic work,
make the life of your Church
ever more fruitful.   Lord, hear our prayer

a) Give in ever greater abundance
    the gifts of the Holy Spirit
    to your servant, Pope N.,
    and to all his brother bishops.   Lord, hear our prayer

b) By the life and labor of all religious
    promote the welfare of all people.   Lord, hear our prayer

b) Lead all men and women
    to the fullness of the Christian life.   Lord, hear our prayer

c) Grant that all religious communities
    may live and grow
    in the love of Christ
    and the spirit of their founders.   Lord, hear our prayer

c) Give to all
    who profess the Gospel counsels
    a fuller share in the work
        of redemption.   Lord, hear our prayer

d) Reward a hundredfold
    the parents of your servants
    for the sacrifice they have made.   Lord, hear our prayer

d) Make these servants of yours
    more and more like Christ,
    the firstborn among many.   Lord, hear our prayer

e) Give these servants of yours
    the grace of perseverance.   Lord, hear our prayer

e) Bless these brothers of ours,
        your servants,
    make them holy,
    and consecrate them to your service.   Lord, hear our prayer

Jesus, Son of the living God	Lord, hear our prayer
Christ, hear us	Christ, hear us
Lord Jesus, hear our prayer	Lord Jesus, hear our prayer

63. Then the celebrant alone rises and says, with hands joined:

Lord,
grant the prayers of your people.
Prepare the hearts of your servants
for consecration to your service.
By the grace of the Holy Spirit
purify them from all sin
and set them on fire with your love.

We ask this through Christ our Lord.

R. Amen.

The deacon then says:

Let us rise.

All stand.

PROFESSION

64. After the litany, if it is the custom of the religious community, two professed religious stand near the celebrant (or superior) to act as witnesses. Those to be professed come, one by one, to the celebrant (or superior) and read the formula of profession, which they themselves have written out beforehand.

65. Then the newly professed may fittingly go to the altar, one by one, to place on it the formula of profession; if it can be done conveniently, each of them should sign the document of profession upon the altar itself. After this, each goes back to his place.

66. Afterward, if this is the practice of the community, the newly professed may stand and sing an antiphon or other song expressing the spirit of self-giving and joy, for example:

Uphold me, Lord, according to your promise
and I shall live;
and do not bring to nothing all my hope (Psalm 119:116).

SOLEMN BLESSING OR CONSECRATION OF THE PROFESSED

67. Then the newly professed kneel; the celebrant with hands extended over them says the prayer of blessing Father in heaven, source of all holiness, *in which the words in parentheses may, to suit the occasion, be* omitted, or else the prayer Lord God, source of holiness and growth in your Church, *which is found in no. 143.*

Father in heaven,
source of all holiness,
creator of the human race,
your love for us was so great
that you gave us a share in your own divine life.
Neither the sin of Adam
nor even the sins of the whole world
could alter your loving purpose.

In the dawn of history
you gave us Abel as an example of holiness.
Later, from your beloved Hebrew people
you raised up men and women graced with every virtue.

Foremost among them all stands Mary,
the ever-virgin daughter of Zion.
From her pure womb was born Jesus Christ,
your eternal Word,
the Savior of the world.

You sent him, Father, as our pattern of holiness.
He became poor to make us rich,
a slave to set us free.
With love no words can tell
he redeemed the world by his paschal mystery
and won from you the gifts of the Spirit
to sanctify his Church.

The voice of the Spirit has drawn
countless numbers of your children
to follow in the footsteps of your Son.
They leave all things
to be one with you in the bonds of love
and give themselves wholly to your service
and the service of all your people.

Look with favor, then,
on these who have heard your call.
Send them the Spirit of holiness;
help them to fulfill in faith
what you have enabled them to promise in joy.
Keep always before their eyes Christ, the divine teacher.

[Give them perfect chastity,
ungrudging poverty
and wholehearted obedience.
May they glorify you by their humility,
serve you with docility,
and be one with you in fervent love.]

May they build up the Church by the holiness of their lives,
advance the salvation of the world,
and stand as a sign of the blessings that are to come.

Lord, protect and guide these servants of yours.
At the judgment seat of your Son
be yourself their great reward.
Give them the joy of vows fulfilled.
Made perfect in your love,
may they rejoice in the communion of your saints
and praise you for ever in their company.

We ask this through Christ our Lord.

R. Amen.

PRESENTATION OF THE INSIGNIA OF PROFESSION

68. *After the blessing of the professed, if it is the custom of the religious community to present insignia of religious profession, the newly professed rise and come before the celebrant, who presents the insignia to each in silence or with a suitable formula.*

69. *Meanwhile the choir and people together sing the antiphon:*

How happy, Lord, are those who dwell in your house,
who sing your praise for ever (Psalm 84:5),

with Psalm 84; or some other appropriate song may be sung. The antiphon is repeated after every two verses; at the end of the psalm Glory to the Father *is not said but only the antiphon. If the presentation of the insignia comes to an end before the whole psalm is sung, the psalm is interrupted and the antiphon repeated.*

STATEMENT OF ADMISSION OR SIGN OF PEACE

70. *When the presentation of the insignia is completed, or after the prayer of solemn blessing, if it is customary or seems opportune, there may be a ceremony to mark the fact that the newly professed religious have been admitted as lifelong members of the institute or religious family. This can take the form of a suitable statement by the celebrant (or superior) or of the sign of peace. For example:*

a) The celebrant (or superior) says these or similar words:

We confirm that you are now one with us
as members of this religious community of N.,
sharing all things in common with us
now and in the future.

He may add:

Be faithful to the ministry the Church entrusts to you
to be carried out in its name.

The members of the community manifest their assent, saying:

R. Amen.

b) The above may be omitted and the celebrant (or superior) and members of the community may give the sign of peace to the newly professed in the usual way or according to the custom of the place. Meanwhile the choir and the people sing the antiphon:

See how good it is, how pleasant,
that brothers live in unity (Psalm 133:1),

with Psalm 133; or some other appropriate song may be sung.

71. *The newly professed religious return after this to their places. The Mass continues.*

LITURGY OF THE EUCHARIST

72. *During the offertory song, some of the newly professed may bring to the altar the bread, wine, and water for the eucharistic sacrifice.*

73. *In the eucharistic prayers, the offering of the professed may be mentioned according to the texts below:*

a) In Eucharistic Prayer I, the special form of Father, accept this offering *is said:*

Father, accept and sanctify this offering
from your whole family and from these your servants
which we make to you on the day of their profession.
By your grace
they have dedicated their lives to you today.
When your Son returns in glory,
may they share the joy of the unending paschal feast.

[Through Christ our Lord. Amen.]

b) In the intercessions of Eucharistic Prayer II, after the words and all the clergy, *there is added:*

Lord, remember also these your brothers
who have today dedicated themselves to serve you always.
Grant that they may always raise their minds and hearts to you
 and glorify your name.

c) In the intercessions of Eucharistic Prayer III, after the words your Son has gained for you, *there is added:*

Strengthen also these your servants in their holy purpose,
for they have dedicated themselves
by the bonds of religious consecration to serve you always.
Grant that they may give witness in your Church
to the new and eternal life won by Christ's redemption.

d) In the intercessions of Eucharistic Prayer IV, the professed may be mentioned in this way:

. . . bishop, and bishops and clergy everywhere.
Remember these our brothers
who unite themselves more closely to you today
by their perpetual profession.
Remember those who take part in this offering . . .

74. *The celebrant gives the sign of peace to each of the newly professed in the usual way, or according to the custom of the place or of the religious community.*

75. *After the celebrant has received the body and blood of Christ, the newly professed religious come to the altar to receive communion which may be given to them under both kinds. Then their parents, relatives, and fellow religious may receive communion in the same way.*

CONCLUDING RITE

SOLEMN BLESSING

76. *When the prayer after communion has been said, the newly consecrated religious stand before the altar, and the celebrant, facing them, may say:*

God inspires all holy desires and brings them to fulfillment.
May he protect you always by his grace
so that you may fulfill the duties of your vocation
with a faithful heart.

R. Amen.

May he make each of you a witness
and sign of his love for all people.

R. Amen.

May he make those bonds,
with which he has bound you to Christ on earth,
endure for ever in heavenly love.

R. Amen.

Another form of the blessing may be found in no. 144.

43

77. *Finally, the celebrant blesses the whole congregation:*

May almighty God,
the Father, and the Son, + and the Holy Spirit,
bless all of you who have taken part in this celebration.

R. Amen.

Chapter IV

RITE FOR RENEWAL
OF VOWS DURING MASS

78. *Renewal of vows, which is governed by the general law of the Church or by a particular ruling of the constitutions, may take place during Mass if the religious community thinks it appropriate.*

79. *The rite for the renewal of vows should be conducted with the greatest simplicity, especially if, in accordance with the constitutions of the religious institute, vows are renewed frequently or annually.*

80. *Either the Mass corresponding to the liturgy of the day or the ritual Mass for the day of the renewal of vows is used, in accordance with the rubrics (see Introduction, no. 9).*

81. *In clerical institutes it is proper for the superior who receives the renewal of vows to preside over the eucharistic sacrifice. In lay institutes a chair should be prepared in a convenient part of the sanctuary for the superior who is to receive the profession of his fellow religious.*

82. *Religious who renew their profession may receive communion under both kinds. If only one chalice is used, it should be sufficiently large.*

OUTLINE OF THE RITE

LITURGY OF THE WORD

RENEWAL OF VOWS
Prayer for God's Grace
Renewal of Profession
General Intercessions

LITURGY OF THE EUCHARIST

RITE FOR RENEWAL
OF VOWS DURING MASS

LITURGY OF THE WORD

83. *In the liturgy of the word, all takes place as usual except for the following:*

a) the readings may be taken from the Mass of the day or from the texts set out in nos. 91-136 (see Introduction, nos. 9-10);

b) the profession of faith may be omitted, even if prescribed by the rubrics of the day.

84. *After the gospel a homily which uses the readings from Scripture to emphasize the meaning and the value of religious life is given.*

RENEWAL OF VOWS

PRAYER FOR GOD'S GRACE

85. *After the homily the celebrant prays for God's help, saying:*

God our Father gives us the grace
　to persevere in our resolutions.
Let us pray to him for these servants of his
who are resolved to renew their vows today
　in the presence of the Church.

All pray for a time in silence. Then the celebrant says:

Lord,
in your providence
you have called these servants of yours
to be perfect as the Gospel teaches.
In your mercy grant that they may persevere to the end
along the way of your love
on which they have set out with such joy.

We ask this through Christ our Lord.

R. Amen.

RENEWAL OF PROFESSION

86. *After the prayer, if it is the custom of the religious community, two professed members of the community stand near the celebrant (or superior) to act as witnesses. Those who are to renew their profession come, one by one, to the celebrant (or superior) and read the formula of profession.*

If there is a large number renewing their vows, the formula of profession may be recited by all. The concluding words, This I promise . . . *or the like, must be said by each individually, as a clear expression of his will.*

GENERAL INTERCESSIONS

87. *The rite fittingly concludes with the recitation of the general intercessions (prayer of the faithful); for these the formula set out in nos. 140-142 may be used.*

LITURGY OF THE EUCHARIST

88. *During the offertory song some of the religious who have renewed their vows may bring the bread, wine, and water to the altar for the eucharistic sacrifice.*

89. *The celebrant, after saying,* "The peace of the Lord," *gives to each of the religious who have renewed their vows the sign of peace in the usual way or in accordance with the custom of the place or of the religious community. If there are many, he gives the sign of peace to the first, who gives it to the rest.*

90. *After the celebrant has received the body and blood of Christ, the religious who have renewed their profession come to the altar to receive communion under both kinds.*

Chapter V

OTHER TEXTS FOR THE RITES
OF RELIGIOUS PROFESSION

I. BIBLICAL READINGS

READINGS FROM THE OLD TESTAMENT

91. *Genesis 12:1-4a* Leave your country, your family, and come.

92. *1 Samuel 3:1-10* Speak, Lord, your servant is listening.

93. *1 Kings 19:4-9a,11-15a* Go out and stand on the mountain before the Lord.

94. *1 Kings 19:16b,19-21* Elisha left and followed Elijah.

READINGS FROM THE NEW TESTAMENT

95. *Acts 2:42-47* All those who believed were equal and held everything in common.

96. *Acts 4:32-35* One heart and one soul.

97. *Romans 6:3-11* Let us walk in newness of life.

98. *Romans 12:1-13* Offer your bodies as a living, holy sacrifice, truly pleasing to God.

99. *1 Corinthians 1:22-31* To many, preaching a crucified Christ is madness; to us it is the power of God.

100. *Ephesians 1:3-14*	The Father chose us in Christ to be holy and spotless in love.
101. *Philippians 2:1-4*	Be united in your convictions and in your love.
102. *Philippians 3:8-14*	I look on everything as useless if only I can know Christ.
103. *Colossians 3:1-4*	Let your thoughts be on heavenly things, not on the things that are on the earth.
104. *Colossians 3:12-17*	Above everything, have love for each other because that is the bond of perfection.
105. *1 Thessalonians 4:1-3a,7-12*	What God wants is for you to be holy.
106. *1 Peter 1:3-9*	You have not seen the Christ, yet you love him.
107. *1 John 4:7-16*	As long as we love one another God will live in us.
108. *Revelation 3:14b,20-22*	I shall share a meal side by side with him.
109. *Revelation 22:12-14,16-17, 20*	Come, Lord Jesus!

RESPONSORIAL PSALMS

110. *Psalm 24:1-2,3-4ab,5-6*
   R. (6): Lord, this is the people that longs to see your face.

111. *Psalm 27:1,4,5,8b-9abc,9d and 11*
   R. (8b): I long to see your face, O Lord.

52

112. *Psalm 33:2-3,4-5,11-12,13-14,18-19,20-21*
    R. (12b):   Happy the people the Lord has
    chosen to be his own.

113. *Psalm 34:2-3,4-5,6-7,8-9 or 10-11,12-13,14-15,17 and 19*
    R. (2a):   I will bless the Lord at all times.
    or (9a):   Taste and see the goodness
    of the Lord.

114. *Psalm 40:2 and 4ab,7-8a,8b-9,10,12*
    R. (8a and 9a):   Here am I, Lord; I come to do
    your will.

115. *Psalm 63:2,3-4,5-6,8-9*
    R. (2b):   My soul is thirsting for you,
    O Lord my God.

116. *Psalm 84:3,4,5-6a and 8a,11,12*
    R. (2):   How lovely is your dwelling place,
    Lord, mighty God!

117. *Psalm 100:2,3,4,5*
    R. (2c):   Come with joy into the presence
    of the Lord.

ALLELUIA VERSE AND VERSE BEFORE THE GOSPEL

118. *Psalm 133:1*
    See how good it is, how pleasant,
    that brothers and sisters live in unity.

119. *Matthew 11:25*
    Blessed are you, Father, Lord of heaven and earth;
    you have revealed to little ones the mysteries of the kingdom.

120. *John 13:34*
    I give you a new commandment:
    love one another as I have loved you.

121. *John 15:5*
    I am the vine and you are the branches, says the Lord:
    those who live in me, and I in them, will bear much fruit.

122. *2 Corinthians 8:9*
    Jesus Christ was rich but he became poor
    to make you rich out of his poverty.

123. *Galatians 6:14*
    My only glory is the cross of our Lord Jesus Christ,
    which crucifies the world to me and me to the world.

124. *Philippians 3:8-9*
    I count all things worthless but this:
    to gain Jesus Christ and to be found in him.

GOSPEL

125. *Matthew 11:25-30*	You have hidden these things from the learned and clever and revealed them to little children.
126. *Matthew 16:24-27*	Any who lose their life for my sake will find it.
127. *Matthew 19:3-12*	There are some persons who choose to remain unmarried for the sake of the kingdom of heaven.
128. *Matthew 19:16-26*	If you wish to be perfect, go and sell everything you have and come, follow me.
129. *Mark 3:31-35*	Whoever does the will of God is my brother, my sister, and my mother.
130. *Mark 10:24b-30*	We have left everything and have followed you.

131. *Luke 9:57-62*	Once the hand is laid on the plow, no one who looks back is fit for the kingdom of God.
132. *Luke 11:27-28*	Happy are they who hear the word of God and keep it.
133. *John 12:24-26*	If a grain of wheat falls on the ground and dies, it yields a rich harvest.
134. *John 15:1-8*	Those who live in me, and I in them, will bear much fruit.
135. *John 15:9-17*	You are friends if you do what I command you.
136. *John 17:20-26*	I want those you have given me to be with me where I am.

II. ANOTHER FORM FOR PRESENTING THE INSIGNIA OF FIRST PROFESSION

PRESENTATION OF THE HABIT

137. *After the profession the celebrant (or superior) assisted by the novice master gives the religious habit to each of the professed with these or similar words:*

Receive this habit as a sign of your consecration.
May you be as closely united to the Lord in your heart
as it proclaims you to be.

The professed replies:

R. Amen.

They put on the habit in some convenient place. After one or two have received the habit the choir may begin the antiphon:

Lord, these are the men who long to see your face,
who seek the face of the God of Jacob (Psalm 24:6),

with Psalm 24; or some other appropriate song may be sung. The antiphon is repeated after every two verses; at the end of the psalm Glory to the Father *is not said but only the antiphon. If the presentation of the insignia comes to an end before the whole psalm is sung, the psalm is interrupted and the antiphon repeated.*

PRESENTATION OF THE RULE OR CONSTITUTIONS

138. *Then, if customary, the newly professed, wearing the religious habit, come to the celebrant (or superior) one by one. He gives the book of the rule or constitutions to each of them, saying these or similar words:*

Receive the rule of our (this) religious community.
By keeping it faithfully, may you arrive at the perfection of love.

The professed replies:

R. Amen.

After receiving the book, he returns to his place and remains standing.

139. *If the newly professed are numerous, or there is some other reason, the celebrant (or superior) may present each of them with the rule and habit and say the formula once for all.*

If, in accordance with the rules or customs of the religious community, other signs of religious profession are to be presented, this is done now in silence or with a suitable formula. In this matter a dignified simplicity should be observed.

III. OPTIONAL GENERAL INTERCESSIONS

INTRODUCTION

140. *a) In the Mass of first profession:*

Dear friends (brothers),
today our community rejoices in the Lord,
because these servants of his desire by their religious profession
to be more generous
in their service of God and of his Church.
Let us in unity of heart pray to God our Father
who gives to each the grace of his vocation.

b) In the Mass of renewal of vows:

Dear friends (brothers),
let us pray to God our Father for his Church,
for the peace and salvation of the world,
for our own community,
and especially for our brothers who have renewed their vows
today.

INTENTIONS

141. *I.* *a)* For the holy Church of God,
that adorned by the virtues of her children
she may shine ever more brightly for Christ,
her Bridegroom:
let us pray to the Lord.

b) For our holy father the Pope and the other bishops,
that by sound teaching and loving care
they may be faithful shepherds of God's holy people:
let us pray to the Lord.

II. *a)* For the peace and salvation of the world,
that all religious may be messengers and servants
of the peace of Christ:
let us pray to the Lord.

b) For the good of all people,
that those who are dedicated to the Lord's service
may pursue the things of heaven
and spend their days in the service of others:
let us pray to the Lord.

c) For all who believe in Christ,
that they may listen attentively to the secret
voice of God
as he invites them all to a life of holiness:
let us pray to the Lord.

d) For the poor and suffering,
that Christ's example may always inspire religious
to bring the good news to the poor,
to care for the sick and to comfort the afflicted:
let us pray to the Lord.

III. *a)* For all religious,
that their way of life
may be a sign to all of the future world to come:
let us pray to the Lord.

b) For those who follow the evangelical counsels,
that the law of love may shine in their lives,
and that like the first disciples
they may be one in heart and mind:
let us pray to the Lord.

c) For all religious,
that each one, according to the call of God,
may increase the holiness of the Church
and work to spread God's kingdom:
let us pray to the Lord.

IV. *a)* For these brothers of ours
who have today bound themselves more closely to God
by religious profession,
that in his goodness he may give them
a love of prayer,
a spirit of penance,
and zeal in the apostolate:
let us pray to the Lord.

b) For these brothers of ours
who have today
bound themselves more closely to God's service,
that their hearts may be filled
with generous love for all:
let us pray to the Lord.

c) For those who today make profession of
the evangelical counsels,
that religious consecration may increase the holiness
to which baptism has called them:
let us pray to the Lord.

d) For those who seek to follow Christ
more closely by religious profession,
that their chastity may show the fruitfulness
  of the Church,
their poverty serve those in need,
and their obedience lead the rebellious
to accept the gentle rule of Christ:
let us pray to the Lord.

e) For all Christ's faithful people,
that the whole Church
may be the light of the world
and the leaven in its midst
to renew society by holy living and hidden prayer:
let us pray to the Lord.

f) For all here present,
that we may be faithful to Christ's teaching
as he calls us to be perfect,
and that we may bear fruit in holiness,
grow into the fullness of Christ,
and meet together in the heavenly city of peace:
let us pray to the Lord.

CONCLUDING PRAYER

142. *a) In the Mass of the first profession:*

Lord,
hear the prayers of your people.
In your goodness you called these servants of yours
to follow Christ and to be perfect.
Through the intercession of the Blessed Virgin Mary,
the mother of the Church,
pour forth your Holy Spirit upon them
so that they may fulfill in their whole lives
the promise they have made today.

We ask this through Christ our Lord.

Lord God,
all holiness is from you.
In your goodness hear the prayers of your family,
and by the intercession of Blessed Mary, your handmaid,
pour forth your blessings in abundance upon these servants
    of yours,
so that by your continued help
they may fulfill the vows
your love has inspired them to renew.

We ask this through Christ our Lord.

R. Amen.

IV. ANOTHER SOLEMN PRAYER OF BLESSING OR CONSECRATION OF THE PROFESSED

143. Lord God,
    source of holiness and growth in your Church,
    all creation owes you its debt of praise.
    In the beginning of time
    you created the world to share your joy.
    When it lay broken by Adam's sin,
    you promised a new heaven and a new earth.
    You entrusted the earth to the care of men and women
    to be made fruitful by their work.
    Living in this world they were to direct their steps
    to the heavenly city.
    By your sacraments
    you make us your children
    and welcome us into your Church;
    you distribute among us
    the many gifts of your Spirit.
    Some serve you in chaste marriage;
    others forego marriage for the sake of your kingdom.
    Sharing all things in common,
    with one heart and mind in the bond of love,
    they become a sign of the communion of heaven.

Father, we pray now,
send your Spirit upon these servants of yours
who have committed themselves
with steadfast faith
to the words of Christ your Son.
Strengthen their understanding
and direct their lives by the teaching of the Gospel.
May the law of love rule in their hearts,
and concern for others distinguish their lives,
so that they may bear witness to you, the one true God,
and to your infinite love for all people.
By their courage in daily trials
may they receive, even in this life,
your promised hundredfold,
and at the end an everlasting reward in heaven.

We ask this through Christ our Lord.

R. Amen.

V. ANOTHER FORM OF BLESSING AT THE END OF THE MASS OF PERPETUAL PROFESSION

144. May God, who is the source of all good intentions,
enlighten your minds and strengthen your hearts.
May he help you to fulfill with steadfast faith
all you have promised.

R. Amen.

May the Lord enable you to travel in the joy of Christ
as you follow along his way,
and may you gladly share each other's burdens.

R. Amen.

May the love of God unite you and make you a true family
praising his name and showing forth Christ's love.

R. Amen.

May almighty God,
the Father, and the Son, + and the Holy Spirit,
bless all of you who have taken part in these sacred celebrations.

R. Amen.

PART II

RITE
OF
RELIGIOUS
PROFESSION
FOR WOMEN

Chapter I

NORMS FOR
THE RITE OF INITIATION
INTO THE RELIGIOUS LIFE

1. *On the day when the canonical novitiate begins, it is fitting that there should be a ceremony to ask God's grace for achieving the special purpose of the novitiate.*

2. *It is forbidden to perform the rite of initiation during Mass.*

3. *The rite is to be very simple and direct, in the presence of the religious community only.*

4. *The texts for the rite must avoid anything that may seem to diminish the novices' freedom of choice or obscure the true meaning of a noviceship or time of testing.*

5. *The chapter hall or other similar room is an appropriate setting for the rite. If it seems necessary, however, the rite may take place in the chapel.*

OUTLINE OF THE RITE

INTRODUCTORY RITES
Greeting or Song
Questioning of the Postulants or Request
for Admission
Prayer

CELEBRATION OF THE WORD OF GOD

CONCLUDING RITES
General Intercessions
Lord's Prayer
Concluding Prayer

RITE OF INITIATION
INTO THE RELIGIOUS LIFE

It is appropriate that the rite should take place during a special celebration of the word on the nature of the religious life and the spirit of the institute.

INTRODUCTORY RITES

GREETING OR SONG

6. *The rite may appropriately begin with a greeting by the superior, or the singing of a psalm or other suitable hymn.*

Questioning of the Postulants or Request for Admission

7. *Then the superior questions the postulants in these or similar words:*

Dear daughters (sisters), what do you ask from us?

The postulants reply together in these or similar words:

We wish to try your way of life,
and are willing to be tested ourselves,
that we may follow Christ wholeheartedly
in this community of N.

The superior replies:

May the Lord grant you his help.

R. Amen.

8. *The questioning may be omitted, and the request for admission takes place as follows: one of the postulants, facing the superior and community, speaks in the name of all:*

Drawn by God's mercy,
we have come here to learn your way of life.
We ask you to teach us to follow Christ crucified
and to live in poverty, obedience and chastity.
Teach us to persevere in prayer and penance,
in the service of the Church and of humankind.
Teach us to be one with you in heart and mind.
Help us to live out the Gospel every day of our lives.
Teach us your rule and help us to learn to love
our sisters as Christ commanded us.

Or she may use similar words, expressing the aspirations and thoughts of the postulants themselves.

The superior responds in these or similar words:

May God in his mercy be with you always,
and may Christ our teacher grant light to us all.

R. Amen.

9. *After the questioning or request for admission, the superior says:*

Let us pray.

Lord God,
you give us the desire to hear your call.
Listen favorably to the prayers of your servants N. and N,
who, desiring to serve you more perfectly,
ask to join our community.
Grant that our life in common
may become a communion of love.

We ask this through Christ our Lord.

R. Amen.

CELEBRATION OF THE WORD OF GOD

10. *Suitable texts from holy Scripture are then read, with appropriate responsories (see nos. 98-152).*

11. *At their conclusion the superior addresses the religious community and the postulants on the meaning of the religious life and the spirit of the institute, or she reads an appropriate chapter of the rule.*

CONCLUDING RITES

12. *The rite fittingly concludes with the general intercessions (prayer of the faithful) and the Lord's Prayer, to which a suitable prayer may be added, such as:*

God our Father,
it is you who have called us.
Hear our prayers and bless these sisters of ours
who wish to follow your Son in religious life.
Help us all to do what you ask of us
so that your plans for them may be fulfilled.

We ask this through Christ our Lord.

R. Amen.

13. *After this the superior entrusts the newly admitted novices to the care of the novice mistress, and with her fellow religious greets them in the spirit of Christian love in the way customary in the religious community. Meanwhile, an appropriate song or a canticle of praise is sung.*

Chapter II

RITE OF
TEMPORARY PROFESSION
DURING MASS

---

14. *The rite described in this chapter takes place during Mass. It may be used only for those religious who make their first profession upon successful completion of the novitiate (see Introduction, no. 5).*

BLESSING OF THE HABIT ON THE DAY BEFORE PROFESSION

15. *It is appropriate to give the religious habit, with the exception of the veil, to the novices the day before their first profession.*

16. *The habits, but not the veils, are blessed by a priest or other competent minister, using this or a similar prayer:*

V. Our help is in the name of the Lord.
R. Who made heaven and earth.

V. The Lord be with you.
R. And also with you.

Let us pray.

God, you clothed your Son with our mortal flesh
in the chaste womb of the Virgin Mary;
give a rich blessing to these habits,
and grant that your servants who wear them on earth
may be a sign of the resurrection to come
and be clothed in the glory of eternal life.

We ask this through Christ our Lord.

R. Amen.

The habits may then be sprinkled with holy water.

17. *At an appropriate time, the superior assembles the community and the novices; in a brief address she prepares the minds of all for the rite of profession to take place the following day. Then she gives the religious habit, with the exception of the veil, to each novice so that she may wear it for the entrance procession at the beginning of Mass.*

18. *The Mass may correspond to the liturgy of the day, or the ritual Mass for the day of first profession may be used, in accordance with the rubrics (see Introduction, nos. 9-11).*

19. *The profession ordinarily takes place at the chair. A chair for the superior who is to receive the sisters' profession should be prepared in a suitable place in the sanctuary. Seats should be so arranged in the sanctuary for those making profession that the faithful may have a complete view of the liturgical rites.*

20. *Religious bound by the law of enclosure may make their temporary profession in the sanctuary, with due respect for the general laws of the Church and the particular occasion.*

21. *Enough bread and wine for consecration should be prepared for the ministers, those making their profession, and their parents, relatives, and fellow religious. If only one chalice is used, it should be sufficiently large.*

22. *In addition to what is needed for Mass, there should also be ready:*

a) the ritual for religious profession;
b) the religious veils, if the religious institute has decided to present them on the occasion of first profession (see Introduction, no. 5);
c) the book of the rule or constitutions, and other insignia of religious profession which, according to law or custom, are to be presented.

OUTLINE OF THE RITE

INTRODUCTORY RITES

LITURGY OF THE WORD

RELIGIOUS PROFESSION
Calling or Request
Homily or Address
Examination
Prayer for God's Grace
Profession
Presentation of the Insignia
   of Religious Profession
      Presentation of the Veil
      Presentation of the Rule or Constitutions
General Intercessions

LITURGY OF THE EUCHARIST

RITE OF
TEMPORARY PROFESSION
DURING MASS

INTRODUCTORY RITES

23. When the people and the religious are assembled and everything is ready, the procession moves through the church to the altar in the usual way, while the choir and people sing the entrance song of the Mass. Those to be professed may fittingly join in the procession, accompanied by the superior and the novice mistress.

24. When they come to the sanctuary all make the customary reverence to the altar and go to their places; then Mass continues.

LITURGY OF THE WORD

25. The liturgy of the word takes place as usual, except for the following:

a) the readings may be taken from the Mass of the day or from the texts in nos. 98-152 (see Introduction, nos. 9-10);

b) the profession of faith may be omitted, even if prescribed by the rubrics of the day.

RELIGIOUS PROFESSION

CALLING OR REQUEST

26. After the gospel the celebrant and the people sit, but those to be professed stand. Then, according to choice or as circumstances demand, the deacon or the novice mistress calls those to be professed by name.

They answer:

Lord, you have called me; here I am,

or they make some other reply according to local usage or the custom of the religious community.

27. The celebrant then questions them in these or similar words:

My dear sisters (daughters), what do you ask of God and of his holy Church?

The candidates reply together in these or similar words:

We ask for God's merciful love
and a share in the life of this religious community of N.

The celebrant and all the members of the religious community reply:

Thanks be to God,

or they express their approval in some other way.

---

28. The calling by name and the questioning by the celebrant may be omitted; a request by those to be professed may take their place. For example, one of those to be professed may stand facing the superior and say, in the name of all, these or similar words:

With the help of God,
we (N. and N.) have studied your rule
and have lived among you as your sisters for the time
   of probation.
Mother (Sister), we now ask to be allowed
to dedicate ourselves to God and his kingdom
by making profession in this religious community of N.

76

The superior and all the members of the religious community reply:

Thanks be to God,

or they express their approval in some other way.

HOMILY OR ADDRESS

29. *Those to be professed then sit and listen to the homily or address which should develop the scriptural readings and the theme of religious profession as God's gift and call for the sanctification of those chosen and for the good of the Church and the whole human family.*

EXAMINATION

30. *After the homily or address, those to be professed stand, and the celebrant questions them on their readiness to dedicate themselves to God and to seek perfect charity, according to the rule or constitutions of the religious community. The questions may be changed or in part omitted, to suit the spirit and character of each religious institute.*

My dear sisters (daughters),
by water and the Holy Spirit
you have already been consecrated to God's service:
are you resolved to unite yourselves more closely to him
by the new bond of religious profession?

They answer:

I am.

The celebrant continues:

In your desire to follow Christ perfectly,
are you resolved to live in chastity
for the sake of the kingdom of heaven,
to choose a life of poverty,
and to offer the sacrifice of obedience?

They answer:

I am.

31. *Then the celebrant confirms their intention in these or similar words:*

May almighty God grant you his grace
to fulfill what you resolve.

R. Amen.

PRAYER FOR GOD'S GRACE

32. *The celebrant then prays for God's help, saying:*

Let us pray.

All pray for a while in silence. Then the celebrant says:

Lord,
look upon these servants of yours
who are resolved to dedicate their lives to you
by making profession of the evangelical counsels
in the presence of your Church today.
Mercifully grant that their manner of life
may bring glory to your name
and further your loving plan of redemption.

We ask this through Christ our Lord.

R. Amen.

PROFESSION

33. *After the prayer, if it is the custom of the religious community, two professed religious stand near the superior to act as witnesses. Those to be professed come, one by one, to the superior and read the formula of profession.*

If there are very many religious making their profession, the formula of profession may be recited by all together. The concluding words, This I promise . . . *or the like, must be said by each individually as a clear expression of her will.*

After the profession, they return to their places and remain standing.

PRESENTATION OF THE INSIGNIA OF RELIGIOUS PROFESSION

PRESENTATION OF THE VEIL

34. After this, if the veil is to be presented, the celebrant, with the assistance of the superior and the mistress of novices, clothes each one with the veil, saying, for example:

Receive this veil
which proclaims
that you belong entirely to Christ the Lord
and are dedicated to the service of the Church.

R. Amen.

PRESENTATION OF THE RULE OR CONSTITUTIONS

35. Then, where it is the custom, the celebrant gives her the book of the rule or constitutions, using this or a similar formula:

Receive the rule of this religious community,
and show in your whole life
what you have faithfully learned.

The professed replies:

R. Amen.

After receiving the book, she returns to her place.

36. After the first or second of the professed has received the veil and rule, the choir intones the antiphon:

I have sought the Lord whom I love with all my heart (Song of Songs 3:4),

with Psalm 45; or some other appropriate song may be sung. The antiphon is repeated after every two verses; at the end of the psalm, Glory to the Father *is not said but only the antiphon. If the presentation of the insignia comes to an end before the whole psalm is sung, the psalm is interrupted and the antiphon repeated.*

37. If, in accordance with the rules or customs of the religious community, other insignia of religious profession are to be presented, this is done now in silence or with a suitable formula. In this matter a dignified simplicity should be observed.

38. *An alternative way of presenting the insignia of profession is described in nos. 153-155.*

GENERAL INTERCESSIONS

39. *The rite fittingly concludes with the general intercessions (prayer of the faithful). For these, the formula given in nos. 156-158 may be used.*

LITURGY OF THE EUCHARIST

40. *During the offertory song, some of the newly professed religious may bring the bread, wine, and water to the altar for the eucharistic sacrifice.*

41. *The celebrant, after saying,* "The peace of the Lord," *gives the sign of peace in some suitable way to the newly professed religious and all those present.*

42. *After the celebrant has received the body and blood of Christ, the newly professed religious come to the altar to receive communion, which may be given to them under both kinds. Then their parents, relatives, and fellow religious may receive communion in the same way.*

Chapter III

RITE OF
PERPETUAL PROFESSION
DURING MASS

---

43. *It is fitting that the rite of profession by which a religious binds herself to God for ever should take place on a Sunday or a solemnity of the Lord, of the Blessed Virgin Mary, or of a saint distinguished in the living of the religious life.*

44. *The rite of perpetual profession takes place separately from other rites of profession (see Introduction, no. 8).*

45. *Notice of the day and hour should be given to the faithful in good time so that they may attend in greater numbers.*

46. *The Mass is that of the liturgy of the day, or the ritual Mass for the day of perpetual profession may be used, in accordance with the rubrics (see Introduction, nos. 9-11).*

47. *Where possible and if the needs of the faithful do not demand individual celebration by the priests present, it is preferable that the Mass be concelebrated.*

48. *The profession ordinarily takes place at the chair. A chair for the superior who is to receive the profession of the sisters should be prepared in a suitable place in the sanctuary. Seats should be so arranged in the sanctuary for those making profession that the faithful may have a complete view of the liturgical rites.*

49. *It is fitting that religious bound by the law of enclosure also make their perpetual profession in the sanctuary.*

50. *Profession ordinarily takes place in the church of the religious community. For pastoral reasons, however, or in order to promote esteem for the religious life, to give edification to the people of God, or to permit larger attendance, the rite may take place in the cathedral, parish church, or some other notable church, as may seem fitting.*

51. *Similarly, where religious from two or more institutes wish to celebrate their profession at the same eucharistic sacrifice, the rite of profession may suitably take place in the cathedral, a parish church, or some other notable church with the bishop presiding. Those making their profession will pronounce their vows before their respective superiors.*

Enclosed religious, however, are to observe carefully the laws of their enclosure in this matter.

52. *As the nature of the rite demands, the whole liturgical service should be celebrated with fitting solemnity, but any appearance of lavishness unbecoming to religious poverty should be avoided.*

53. *Enough bread and wine for consecration should be prepared for the ministers, those making their profession, and their parents, relatives, and fellow religious. If only one chalice is used, it should be sufficiently large.*

54. *In addition to what is needed for Mass, there should also be ready:*

a) the ritual for religious profession;
b) the rings and other insignia of religious profession, if these are to be presented in accordance with the rules or customs of the religious community.

OUTLINE OF THE RITE

INTRODUCTORY RITES

LITURGY OF THE WORD

RELIGIOUS PROFESSION
Calling or Request
Homily or Address
Examination
Litany
Profession
Solemn Blessing or Consecration
   of the Professed
Presentation of the Insignia of Profession
Statement of Admission or Sign of Peace

LITURGY OF THE EUCHARIST

CONCLUDING RITE
Solemn Blessing

RITE OF
PERPETUAL PROFESSION
DURING MASS

INTRODUCTORY RITES

55. *When the people and the religious are assembled and everything is ready, the procession moves through the church to the altar in the usual way, while the choir and people sing the entrance song of the Mass. Those to be professed may join in the procession, accompanied by the superior and the novice mistress.*

56. *When they come to the sanctuary, all make the customary reverence to the altar and go to their places; then Mass continues.*

LITURGY OF THE WORD

57. *The liturgy of the word takes place as usual, except for the following:*

a) the readings may be taken from the Mass of the day or from the texts in nos. 98-152 (see Introduction, nos. 9-10);

b) the profession of faith may be omitted, even if prescribed by the rubrics of the day.

c) the general intercessions in the form customarily used during the celebration of Mass are omitted (see no. 67).

RELIGIOUS PROFESSION

CALLING OR REQUEST

58. After the gospel the celebrant and the people sit, but those to be professed stand. Then, according to choice or as circumstances demand, the deacon or the novice mistress calls those to be professed by name.

They answer:

Lord, you have called me; here I am,

or they make some other reply according to local usage or the custom of the religious community.

59. The celebrant then questions them in these or similar words:

My dear sisters (daughters), what do you ask of God and of his holy Church?

The candidates reply together in these or similar words:

We ask for perseverance
in following Christ our Bridegroom
in this religious community
all the days of our lives.

The celebrant, superior, and all the members of the religious community reply:

Thanks be to God,

or they express their approval in some other way.

60. The calling by name and the questioning by the celebrant may be omitted; a request by those to be professed may take their place. For example, one of those to be professed may stand facing the superior and say, in the name of all, these or similar words:

With the help of God,
we (N. and N.) have come to know in your religious community
the difficulty and the joy of a life completely dedicated to him.
Mother (Sister), we now ask to be allowed
to make perpetual profession in this community of N.
for the glory of God and the service of the Church.

The superior and all the members of the religious community reply:

Thanks be to God,

or they express their approval in some other way.

HOMILY OR ADDRESS

61. *Those to be professed then sit and listen to the homily or address which should develop the scriptural readings and the theme of religious profession as God's gift and call for the sanctification of those chosen and for the good of the Church and the whole human family.*

EXAMINATION

62. *After the homily or address, those to be professed stand, and the celebrant questions them on their readiness to dedicate themselves to God and to seek perfect charity, according to the rule or constitutions of the religious community. The questions may be changed or in part omitted, to suit the spirit and character of each religious institute.*

Dear sisters (daughters),
in baptism you have already died to sin
and have been set aside for God's service.
Are you now resolved to unite yourself more closely to God
by the bond of perpetual profession?

They answer:

I am.

The celebrant continues:

Are you resolved,
with the help of God,
to undertake that life of perfect chastity, obedience, and poverty
chosen for themselves by Christ our Lord and his Virgin Mother,
and to persevere in it for ever?

They answer:

I am.

The celebrant continues:

Are you resolved to strive steadfastly for perfection
in the love of God and of your neighbor
by living the Gospel with all your heart
and keeping the rule of this religious community?

They answer:

I am.

The celebrant continues:

Are you resolved,
with the help of the Holy Spirit,
to spend your whole life in the generous
  service of God's people?

They answer:

I am.

63. *In the case of religious communities wholly dedicated to the
contemplative life, this may appropriately be added:*

The celebrant asks:

Are you resolved to live for God alone,
in solitude and silence,
in persevering prayer and willing penance,
in humble work and holiness of life?

They answer:

I am.

64. *At the end of the questions, the celebrant confirms the intention of those to be professed in these or similar words:*

May God who has begun the good work in you
bring it to fulfillment
before the day of Christ Jesus.

All:

Amen.

LITANY

65. *All then rise. The celebrant stands, with hands joined, and says, facing the people:*

Dear friends in Christ,
let us pray to God the almighty Father
who gives us everything that is good:
in his mercy may he strengthen his servants
in the purpose he has inspired in them.

66. *The deacon gives the sign to kneel.*

Let us kneel.

The celebrant, at his chair, the ministers, those to be professed and the people kneel. Where there is the custom of prostration of those to be professed, this may be kept. During the Easter Season and on all Sundays, all stand except those to be professed.

67. *Then the cantors sing the litany for the rite of religious profession, all making the responses. In this litany one or the other of the petitions marked with the same letter may be omitted. At the appropriate place there may be inserted invocations of saints especially venerated in the religious community or by the faithful; other petitions may be added to suit the occasion.*

Lord, have mercy	Lord, have mercy
Christ, have mercy	Christ, have mercy
Lord, have mercy	Lord, have mercy
Holy Mary, Mother of God	pray for us
Saint Michael	pray for us
Holy angels of God	pray for us
Saint John the Baptist	pray for us
Saint Joseph	pray for us
Saint Peter and Saint Paul	pray for us
Saint John	pray for us
Saint Mary Magdalene	pray for us
Saint Stephen and Saint Lawrence	pray for us
Saint Agnes	pray for us
Saint Basil	pray for us

Saint Augustine	pray for us
Saint Benedict	pray for us
Saint Bernard	pray for us
Saint Francis and Saint Dominic	pray for us
Saint Macrina	pray for us
Saint Scholastica	pray for us
Saint Clare and Saint Catherine	pray for us
Saint Teresa of Jesus	pray for us
Saint Rose of Lima	pray for us
Saint Jane Frances de Chantal	pray for us
Saint Louise de Marillac	pray for us
All holy men and women	pray for us

Lord, be merciful	Lord, save your people
From all evil	Lord, save your people
From every sin	Lord, save your people
From everlasting death	Lord, save your people
By your coming as man	Lord, save your people
By your death and rising to new life	Lord, save your people
By your gift of the Holy Spirit	Lord, save your people

Be merciful to us sinners	Lord, hear our prayer

a) By the self-offering of your servants
and their apostolic work,
make the life of your Church
ever more fruitful.   Lord, hear our prayer

a) Give in ever greater abundance
the gifts of the Holy Spirit
to your servant, Pope N.,
and to all his brother bishops.   Lord, hear our prayer

b) By the life and labor of all religious
promote the welfare of all people. Lord, hear our prayer

b) Lead all men and women
to the fullness of the Christian life. Lord, hear our prayer

90

c) Grant that all religious families
    may live and grow
    in the love of Christ
    and the spirit of their founders.   Lord, hear our prayer

c) Give to all
    who profess the Gospel counsels
    a fuller share in the work of
        redemption.   Lord, hear our prayer

d) Reward a hundredfold
    the parents of your servants
    for the sacrifice they have made.   Lord, hear our prayer

d) Make these servants of yours
    more and more like Christ,
    the firstborn among many.   Lord, hear our prayer

e) Give these servants of yours
    the grace of perseverance.   Lord, hear our prayer

e) Bless these sisters of ours,
        your servants,
    make them holy,
    and consecrate them to your service.   Lord, hear our prayer

    Jesus, Son of the living God   Lord, hear our prayer
    Christ, hear us   Christ, hear us
    Lord Jesus, hear our prayer   Lord Jesus, hear our prayer

68. *Then the celebrant alone rises and says, with hands joined:*

Lord,
grant the prayers of your people.
Prepare the hearts of your servants
for consecration to your service.

By the grace of the Holy Spirit
purify them from all sin
and set them on fire with your love.

We ask this through Christ our Lord.

R. Amen.

The deacon then says:

Let us rise.

All stand.

PROFESSION

69. *After the litany, if it is the custom of the religious community, two professed members of the community come to the chair of the superior and, standing, act as witnesses. Those to be professed come, one by one, to the superior and read the formula of profession, which they themselves have written out beforehand.*

70. *Then the newly professed may fittingly go to the altar, one by one, to place on it the formula of profession; if it can be done conveniently, each of them should sign the document of profession upon the altar itself. After this, each goes back to her place.*

71. *Afterward, if this is the practice of the community, the newly professed may stand and sing an antiphon or other song expressing the spirit of self-giving and joy, for example:*

Uphold me, Lord, according to your promise
and I shall live;
and do not bring to nothing all my hope (Psalm 119:116).

SOLEMN BLESSING OR CONSECRATION OF THE PROFESSED

72. Then the newly professed kneel; the celebrant with hands extended over them says the prayer of blessing Father in heaven, our desire to serve you, *in which the words in parentheses may, to suit the occasion, be omitted, or else the prayer* Lord God, creator of the world and Father of mankind, *which is found in no. 159.*

Father in heaven,
our desire to serve you is itself your gift
and our perseverance needs your guiding hand.
How right it is that we should sing your praise.

With boundless love
you created the human family
through your Word, in the Holy Spirit,
and lifted it up into communion with yourself;
you make the human family your bride
radiant with your own likeness,
adorned with the gifts of everlasting life.

When your bride, deceived by the evil one,
broke faith with you,
you did not abandon her.
With everlasting love you renewed with your servant Noah
the covenant you made with Adam.
[Then you chose Abraham, the man of faith,
to be the father of a people
more numerous than the stars of heaven.
By the hand of Moses
you sealed a covenant with them in the tables of the law.
Throughout the ages
there arose from this favored people
holy women renowned for devotion and courage,
justice and faith.]

In the fullness of time
you raised up the Holy Virgin from the stock of Jesse.
The Holy Spirit was to come upon her,
and your power was to overshadow her,
making her the immaculate Mother of the world's Redeemer.

He became poor, humble, and obedient,
the source and pattern of all holiness.
He formed the Church into his bride,
loving it with love so great
that he gave himself up for it
and sanctified it in his blood.

Father, in your loving wisdom
you have singled out many of your daughters
to be disciples espoused to Christ
and to receive the honor of his love.
[Holy Church shines with their rich variety,
a bride adorned with jewels,
a queen robed in grace,
a mother rejoicing in her children.]

Father, we earnestly pray you:
send the fire of the Holy Spirit
into the hearts of your daughters
to keep alive within them
the holy desire he has given them.

Lord, may the glory of baptism and holiness of life
shine in their hearts.
Strengthened by the vows of their consecration,
may they be always one with you
in loving fidelity to Christ, their only Bridegroom.
May they cherish the Church as their mother
and love the whole world as God's creation,
teaching all people to look forward in joy and hope
to the good things of heaven.

Lord, holy Father,
guide the steps of your servants
and guard them on their pilgrimage through life.
When they come at last to the throne of Christ the King,
may they not fear him as their judge,
but hear the voice of their Bridegroom
lovingly inviting them to the wedding feast of heaven.

We ask this through Christ our Lord.

R. Amen.

PRESENTATION OF THE INSIGNIA OF PROFESSION

73. After the blessing of the professed, the celebrant and the people sit; if rings are to be presented, the newly professed rise and come to the celebrant, who gives the ring to each, saying, for example:

Receive this ring,
for you are betrothed to the eternal King;
keep faith with your Bridegroom
so that you may come to the wedding feast of eternal joy.

The professed replies:

Amen.

Then she returns to her place.

74. If there are several newly professed, or if there is any other good reason, the celebrant may use one formula for presenting the rings to all:

Receive this ring,
for you are betrothed to the eternal King;
keep faith with your Bridegroom
so that you may come to the wedding feast of eternal joy.

They reply:

Amen.

Then they go to the celebrant to receive the rings.

75. Meanwhile the choir and people together sing this or some other suitable antiphon:

I am betrothed to the Son of the eternal Father,
to him who was born of the Virgin Mother
to be the Savior of all the world,

with Psalm 45; or some other appropriate song may be sung. The antiphon is repeated after every two verses; at the end of the psalm Glory to the Father *is not said but only the antiphon. If the presentation of the insignia comes to an end before the whole psalm is sung, the psalm is interrupted and the antiphon repeated.*

76. If, in accordance with the laws or customs of the religious community, other insignia of religious profession are to be presented, this is done now, in silence or with a suitable formula. In this matter a dignified simplicity should be observed.

STATEMENT OF ADMISSION OR SIGN OF PEACE

77. After this, if it is customary or seems opportune, there may be a ceremony to mark the fact that the newly professed religious have been admitted as lifelong members of the religious family. This can take the form of a suitable statement by the superior or of the sign of peace. For example:

a) The superior says these or similar words:

We confirm that you are now one with us
as members of this religious community of N.,
sharing all things in common with us
now and in the future.

She may add:

Be faithful to the ministry the Church entrusts to you
to be carried out in its name.

The members of the community manifest their assent, saying:

R. Amen.

b) The above may be omitted and the celebrant may give the sign of peace. The superior and the members of the community express fraternal love for the newly professed by the sign of peace or in another way, according to the custom of the religious community. Meanwhile the choir and the people sing the antiphon:

How lovely is your dwelling place, Lord, mighty God!
My soul is longing and fainting for the courts of the Lord
(Psalm 84:2-3),

with Psalm 84; or some other appropriate song may be sung.

78. The newly professed religious return after this to their places. The Mass continues.

LITURGY OF THE EUCHARIST

79. *During the offertory song, some of the newly professed may bring to the altar the bread, wine, and water for the eucharistic sacrifice.*

80. *In the eucharistic prayers, the offering of the professed may be mentioned according to the texts below:*

a) In Eucharistic Prayer I, the special form of Father, accept this offering *is said:*

Father, accept and sanctify this offering
from your whole family and from these your servants
which we make to you on the day of their consecration.
By your grace
they join themselves more closely to your Son today.
When he comes in glory at the end of time,
may they joyfully meet him.

[Through Christ our Lord. Amen.]

b) In the intercessions of Eucharistic Prayer II, after the words and all the clergy, *there is added:*

Remember all these sisters of ours
who have left all things for your sake,
so that they may find you in all things
and by forgetting self serve the needs of all.

c) In the intercessions of Eucharistic Prayer III, after the words your Son has gained for you, *there is added:*

Lord, strengthen these servants of yours in their holy purpose,
as they strive to follow Christ your Son in consecrated holiness
by giving witness to his love in their religious life.

d) In the intercessions of Eucharistic Prayer IV, the professed may be mentioned in this way:

. . . bishop, and bishops and clergy everywhere.
Remember our sisters who have consecrated themselves
    to you today
by the bond of religious profession.
Remember those who take part in this offering . . .

81. *The celebrant gives the sign of peace in some suitable form to the newly professed religious and to all those present.*

82. *After the celebrant has received the body and blood of Christ, the newly professed religious come to the altar to receive communion which may be given to them under both kinds. Then their parents, relatives, and fellow religious may receive communion in the same way.*

CONCLUDING RITE

SOLEMN BLESSING

83. *When the prayer after communion has been said, the newly consecrated religious stand before the altar, and the celebrant, facing them, may say:*

God inspires all holy desires and brings them to fulfillment.
May he protect you always by his grace
so that you may fulfill the duties of your vocation
with a faithful heart.

R. Amen.

May he make each of you a witness
and sign of his love for all people.

R. Amen.

May he make those bonds,
with which he has bound you to Christ on earth,
endure for ever in heavenly love.

R. Amen.

Another form of the blessing may be found in no. 160.

84. *Finally, the celebrant blesses the whole congregation:*

May almighty God,
the Father, and the Son, + and the Holy Spirit,
bless all of you who have taken part in this celebration.

R. Amen.

Chapter IV

RITE FOR RENEWAL
OF VOWS DURING MASS

85. *Renewal of vows, which is governed by the general law of the Church or by a particular ruling of the constitutions, may take place during Mass if the religious community thinks it appropriate.*

86. *The rite for the renewal of vows should be conducted with the greatest simplicity, especially if, in accordance with the constitutions of the religious institute, vows are renewed frequently or annually.*

87. *Either the Mass corresponding to the liturgy of the day or the ritual Mass for the day of the renewal of vows is used, in accordance with the rubrics (see Introduction, nos. 9-10).*

88. *The renewal of vows customarily takes place before the superior, whose chair may be placed in a suitable place in the sanctuary.*

89. *Religious who renew their profession may receive communion under both kinds. If only one chalice is used, it should be sufficiently large.*

OUTLINE OF THE RITE

LITURGY OF THE WORD

RENEWAL OF VOWS
Prayer for God's Grace
Renewal of Profession
General Intercessions

LITURGY OF THE EUCHARIST

RITE FOR RENEWAL
OF VOWS DURING MASS

LITURGY OF THE WORD

90. *In the liturgy of the word, all takes place as usual except for the following:*

a) the readings may be taken from the Mass of the day or from the texts set out in nos. 98-152 (see Introduction, nos. 9-10);

b) the profession of faith may be omitted, even if prescribed by the rubrics of the day.

91. *After the gospel a homily which uses the readings from Scripture to emphasize the meaning and the value of religious life is given.*

RENEWAL OF VOWS

PRAYER FOR GOD'S GRACE

92. *After the homily the celebrant prays for God's help, saying:*

God our Father gives us the grace
    to persevere in our resolutions.
Let us pray to him for these servants of his
who are resolved to renew their vows today
    in the presence of the Church.

All pray for a time in silence. Then the celebrant says:

Lord,
in your providence
you have called these servants of yours
to follow your Son more closely.
Mercifully grant that they may persevere to the end
along the way of your love
on which they have set out with such joy.

We ask this through Christ our Lord.

R. Amen.

RENEWAL OF PROFESSION

93. *After the prayer, if it is the custom of the religious community, two professed sisters stand near the superior to act as witnesses.*

Those who are to renew their profession come, one by one, to the superior and read the formula of profession. If there is a large number renewing their vows, the formula of profession may be recited by all. The concluding words, This I promise . . . *or the like, must be said by each individually, as a clear expression of her will.*

Where profession is renewed by all each year, in accordance with the constitutions of the institute, the superior and all the sisters should recite the formula of profession together.

GENERAL INTERCESSIONS

94. *The rite fittingly concludes with the recitation of the general intercessions (prayer of the faithful); for these the formula set out in nos. 156-158 may be used.*

LITURGY OF THE EUCHARIST

95. *During the offertory song some of the religious who have renewed their vows may bring the bread, wine, and water to the altar for the eucharistic sacrifice.*

96. *The celebrant, after saying,* "The peace of the Lord," *gives the sign of peace in a suitable way to the religious who have just renewed their profession and to all those present.*

97. *After the celebrant has received the body and blood of Christ, the religious who have renewed their profession come to the altar to receive communion under both kinds.*

Chapter V

OTHER TEXTS
FOR THE RITES
OF RELIGIOUS PROFESSION

I. BIBLICAL READINGS

READINGS FROM THE OLD TESTAMENT

98.	*Genesis 12:1-4a*	Leave your country, your family, and come.
99.	*1 Samuel 3:1-10*	Speak, Lord, your servant is listening.
100.	*1 Kings 19:4-9a,11-15a*	Go out and stand on the mountain before the Lord.
101.	*1 Kings 19:16b,19-21*	Elisha left and followed Elijah.
102.	*Song of Songs 2:8-14*	Rise, my love, and come.
103.	*Song of Songs 8:6-7*	Love is strong as death.
104.	*Isaiah 61:9-11*	I exult for joy in the Lord.
105.	*Hosea 2:14,19-20 (Hebrew 16,21-22)*	I will betroth you to myself for ever.

READINGS FROM THE NEW TESTAMENT

106.	*Acts 2:42-47*	All those who believed were equal and held everything in common.

107. *Acts 4:32-35*	One heart and one soul.
108. *Romans 6:3-11*	Let us walk in newness of life.
109. *Romans 12:1-13*	Offer your bodies as a living, holy sacrifice, truly pleasing to God.
110. *1 Corinthians 1:22-31*	To many, preaching a crucified Christ is madness; to us it is the power of God.
111. *1 Corinthians 7:25-35*	An unmarried woman can devote herself to the Lord's work.
112. *Ephesians 1:3-14*	The Father chose us in Christ to be holy and spotless in love.
113. *Philippians 2:1-4*	Be united in your convictions and in your love.
114. *Philippians 3:8-14*	I look on everything as useless if only I can know Christ.
115. *Colossians 3:1-4*	Let your thoughts be on heavenly things, not on the things that are on the earth.
116. *Colossians 3:12-17*	Above everything, have love for each other because that is the bond of perfection.
117. *1 Thessalonians 4:1-3a,7-12*	What God wants is for you to be holy.
118. *1 Peter 1:3-9*	You have not seen the Christ, yet you love him.
119. *1 John 4:7-16*	As long as we love one another God will live in us.
120. *Revelation 3:14b,20-22*	I shall share a meal side by side with him.
121. *Revelation 22:12-14,16-17, 20*	Come, Lord Jesus!

RESPONSORIAL PSALMS

122. *Psalm 24:1-2,3-4ab,5-6*
    R. (6): Lord, this is the people that longs to see your face.

123. *Psalm 27:1,4,5,8b-9abc,9d and 11*
    R. (8b): I long to see your face, O Lord.

124. *Psalm 33:2-3,4-5,11-12,13-14,18-19,20-21*
    R. (12b): Happy the people the Lord has chosen to be his own.

125. *Psalm 34:2-3,4-5,6-7,8-9 or 10-11,12-13,14-15,17 and 19*
    R. (2a): I will bless the Lord at all times.
    or (9a): Taste and see the goodness of the Lord.

126. *Psalm 40:2 and 4ab,7-8a,8b-9,10,12*
    R. (8a and 9a): Here am I, Lord; I come to do your will.

127. *Psalm 45:11-12,14-15,16-17*
    R. (Matthew 25:6): The Bridegroom is here; let us go out to meet Christ the Lord.

128. *Psalm 63:2,3-4,5-6,8-9*
    R. (2b): My soul is thirsting for you, O Lord my God.

129. *Psalm 84:3,4,5-6a and 8a,11,12*
    R. (2): How lovely is your dwelling place, Lord, mighty God!

130. *Psalm 100:2,3,4,5*
    R. (2c): Come with joy into the presence of the Lord.

ALLELUIA VERSE AND VERSE BEFORE THE GOSPEL

131. *Psalm 133:1*
See how good it is, how pleasant,
that brothers and sisters live in unity.

132. *Matthew 11:25*
Blessed are you, Father, Lord of heaven and earth;
you have revealed to little ones the mysteries of the kingdom.

133. *John 13:34*
I give you a new commandment:
love one another as I have loved you.

134. *John 15:5*
I am the vine and you are the branches, says the Lord:
those who live in me, and I in them, will bear much fruit.

135. *2 Corinthians 8:9*
Jesus Christ was rich but he became poor
to make you rich out of his poverty.

136. *Galatians 6:14*
My only glory is the cross of our Lord Jesus Christ,
which crucifies the world to me and me to the world.

137. *Philippians 3:8-9*
I count all things worthless but this:
to gain Jesus Christ and to be found in him.

GOSPEL

138. *Matthew 11:25-30*
You have hidden these things from the learned and clever and revealed them to little children.

139. *Matthew 16:24-27*
Any who lose their life for my sake will find it.

140. *Matthew 19:3-12*
There are some persons who choose to remain unmarried for the sake of the kingdom of heaven.

141. *Matthew 19:16-26*	If you wish to be perfect, go and sell everything you have and come, follow me.
142. *Matthew 25:1-13*	Look, the Bridegroom is coming; go out and meet him.
143. *Mark 3:31-35*	Whoever does the will of God is my brother, my sister, and my mother.
144. *Mark 10:24b-30*	We have left everything and have followed you.
145. *Luke 1:26-38*	I am the handmaid of the Lord.
146. *Luke 9:57-62*	Once the hand is laid on the plow, no one who looks back is fit for the kingdom of God.
147. *Luke 10:38-42*	Jesus accepts the hospitality of Martha and praises the attentiveness of Mary.
148. *Luke 11:27-28*	Happy are they who hear the word of God and keep it.
149. *John 12:24-26*	If a grain of wheat falls on the ground and dies, it yields a rich harvest.
150. *John 15:1-8*	Those who live in me, and I in them, will bear much fruit.
151. *John 15:9-17*	You are friends if you do what I command you.
152. *John 17:20-26*	I want those you have given me to be with me where I am.

II. ANOTHER FORM FOR PRESENTING THE INSIGNIA OF FIRST PROFESSION

PRESENTATION OF THE VEIL AND RULE

153. If there are many newly professed religious, or if there is any other good reason, the celebrant presenting the insignia of profession uses this formula once for all:

Receive, dear sisters,
this veil and rule
which are the signs of your profession.
Give yourselves wholeheartedly to Christ the Lord,
and show in your whole life
what you have faithfully learned.

The professed reply:

R. Amen.

They come to the celebrant who, with the assistance of the superior and the mistress of novices, gives to each of them the veil and the book of the rule.

When they have received them they return to their places.

154. Meanwhile, the choir intones the antiphon:

I have sought the Lord whom I love with all my heart (Song of Songs 3:4),

with Psalm 45; or some other appropriate song may be sung. At the end of the psalm Glory to the Father is not said but only the antiphon. If the presentation of the insignia comes to an end before the whole psalm is sung, the psalm is interrupted and the antiphon repeated.

155. If, in accordance with the rules or customs of the religious community, other insignia of religious profession are to be presented, this is done now in silence or with a suitable formula. In this matter a dignified simplicity should be observed.

III. OPTIONAL GENERAL INTERCESSIONS

INTRODUCTION

156. *a) In the Mass of first profession:*

Dear friends,
as we celebrate the paschal mystery of Christ
and the first profession of these sisters,
let us pray together to God the almighty Father,
through Jesus Christ, the inspiration of religious life.

b) In the Mass of renewal of vows:

Dear friends,
Christ our Lord has told us,
"Without me you can do nothing."
Let us pray through him to the Father of all mercies
for the salvation of all people,
for peace in our time,
and for these sisters of ours who renew their vows today.

INTENTIONS

157. *I.* *a)*   For the holy Church of God,
that adorned by the virtues of her children
she may shine ever more brightly for Christ,
her Bridegroom:
let us pray to the Lord.

b)   For our holy father the Pope and the other bishops,
that the Holy Spirit who filled the apostles
may pour out his grace unceasingly upon
their successors:
let us pray to the Lord.

c)   For all those who minister to the Church,
that by word and work
they may lead to salvation
the people entrusted to their care:
let us pray to the Lord.

II. *a)*   For the peace and salvation of the world,
that all religious may be messengers and servants
of the peace of Christ:
let us pray to the Lord.

    b)   For the good of all people,
that those who are dedicated to the Lord's service
may pursue the things of heaven
and spend their days in the service of others:
let us pray to the Lord.

    c)   For all who believe in Christ,
that they may listen attentively to the secret
voice of God
as he invites them all to a life of holiness:
let us pray to the Lord.

III. *a)*   For all religious,
that they may offer
spiritual sacrifices to God with heart and tongue,
with hand and mind,
in labor and suffering:
let us pray to the Lord.

    b)   For those who follow the evangelical counsels,
that the law of love may shine in their lives,
and that like the first disciples
they may be one in heart and mind:
let us pray to the Lord.

    c)   For all who are consecrated to God in religion
that they may share in the life of the Church
and cooperate fully in all her works and hopes:
let us pray to the Lord.

    d)   For all religious,
that each one, according to the call of God,
may increase the holiness of the Church
and work to spread God's kingdom:
let us pray to the Lord.

IV. *a)* For these sisters of ours
who have today bound themselves more closely to God
by religious profession,
that in his goodness he may give them
    a love of prayer,
a spirit of penance,
and zeal in the apostolate:
let us pray to the Lord.

b) For these sisters of ours
who have today
bound themselves more closely to God's service,
that their hearts may be filled
with generous love for all:
let us pray to the Lord.

c) For these sisters of ours
who have today dedicated themselves
to Christ the Lord,
that, like the wise virgins,
they may keep alight the lamp of faith and love:
let us pray to the Lord.

d) For these religious
who have today sealed their desire for holiness,
that they may keep watch for the Bridegroom,
and so enter the wedding feast of heaven:
let us pray to the Lord. .

e) For those who today make profession of
    the evangelical counsels,
that religious consecration may increase the holiness
to which baptism has called them:
let us pray to the Lord.

f) For all here present,
that we may be faithful to Christ's teaching
as he calls us to be perfect,
and that we may bear fruit in holiness,
grow into the fullness of Christ,
and meet together in the heavenly city of peace:
let us pray to the Lord.

CONCLUDING PRAYER

158. *a) In the Mass of the first profession:*

Lord, protect your family,
and in your goodness grant our prayers
for these sisters of ours
as they offer you the first fruits
of their consecrated lives.

We ask this through Christ our Lord.

R. Amen.

b) In the Mass of renewal of vows:

Lord God,
you are the source of truth and mercy.
Hear the prayers of your people,
and by the intercession of the Blessed Virgin Mary,
    Mother of God,
pour into these your servants
the strength to persevere,
so that by following you faithfully
they may fulfill the vows which they now renew.

We ask this through Christ our Lord.

R. Amen.

IV. ANOTHER SOLEMN PRAYER OF BLESSING OR CONSECRATION OF THE PROFESSED

159. Lord God, creator of the world and Father of humankind,
we honor you with praise and thanksgiving,
for you chose a people from the stock of Abraham
and consecrated them to yourself,
calling them by your name.
While they wandered in the wilderness
your word gave them comfort
and your right hand protection.

When they were poor and despised,
you united them to yourself in a covenant of love.
When they strayed from your friendship
your mercy led them back to the right way.
When they sought you,
your fatherly care looked after them
until they came to dwell in the land of freedom.

But above all, Father, we thank you
for revealing the knowledge of your truth
through Jesus Christ, your Son, our brother.

Born of the Blessed Virgin,
by dying he ransomed your people from sin,
and by rising again he showed them the glory
that would one day be their own.

When he took his place at your right hand,
he sent the Holy Spirit to call countless disciples
to follow the evangelical counsels
and consecrate their lives to the glory of your name
and the salvation of all.

Today it is right
that your house should echo with a new song of thanksgiving
for these sisters of ours
who have listened to your voice
and made themselves over to your holy service.

Lord, send the gift of your Holy Spirit upon your servants
who have left all things for your sake.
Father, may their lives reveal the face of Christ your Son,
so that all who see them may come to know
that he is always present in your Church.

We pray that in the freedom of their hearts
they may free from care the hearts of others;
in helping the afflicted, may they bring comfort to Christ
suffering in his brothers and sisters;
may they look upon the world
and see it ruled by your loving wisdom.
May the gift they make of themselves
hasten the coming of your kingdom,
and make them one at last with your saints in heaven.

We ask this through Christ our Lord.

R. Amen.

V. ANOTHER FORM OF BLESSING AT THE END OF THE MASS OF PERPETUAL PROFESSION

160. May the almighty Father make you firm in faith,
innocent in the midst of evil,
and wise in the pursuit of goodness.

R. Amen.

May the Lord Jesus, whom you follow,
enable you to live out the mystery
of his death and resurrection in your own life.

R. Amen.

May the fire of the Holy Spirit
cleanse your hearts from all sin
and set them on fire with his love.

R. Amen.

May almighty God,
the Father, and the Son, + and the Holy Spirit,
bless all of you who have taken part in these sacred celebrations.

R. Amen.

APPENDIX

APPENDIX

I. A SAMPLE FORMULA OF PROFESSION

Each religious community may compose a formula of profession, to be approved by the Sacred Congregation for Religious and for Secular Institutes. For the convenience of religious institutes the following example is given.

1. *Candidates for profession:*

I, N.,
for the glory of God,
and intending to consecrate myself more closely to him
and to follow Christ more generously all my life,
with (Bishop N., and) my brothers (sisters) as witnesses
and in your presence, N.,[1]
vow perpetual[2] chastity, poverty, and obedience
according to the (rule and) constitutions of N.[3]
With my whole heart I give myself
to this religious community,
to seek perfect charity
in the service of God and the Church,
by the grace of the Holy Spirit
and the prayers of the Blessed Virgin Mary.

2. *The person who receives the vows may at a suitable point in the rite (see Part I, no. 70; Part II, no. 77) say the following:*

By the authority entrusted to me,
and in the name of the Church,
I receive the vows you have taken
in the community of N.[3]

---

[1] Here are mentioned the name and office of the superior receiving the profession.

[2] Or the period of tempory profession.

[3] The name of the religious community is mentioned.

I earnestly commend you to God,
that your gift of self,
made one with the sacrifice of the Eucharist,
may be brought to perfection.

II. TEXTS FOR MASS

This Mass may be said on any day except the Sundays of Advent, Lent and Easter, solemnities, Ash Wednesday and the weekdays of Holy Week. White vestments may be worn.

1. FIRST RELIGIOUS PROFESSION

Introductory Rites

Here am I, Lord; I come to do your will. Your law is written on my heart (Psalm 40:8-9).

OPENING PRAYER

Lord,
you have inspired our brothers (sisters)
with the resolve to follow Christ more closely.
Grant a blessed ending to the journey
on which they have set out,
so that they may be able to offer you
the perfect gift of their loving service.

We ask this through our Lord Jesus Christ, your Son,
who lives and reigns with you and the Holy Spirit,
one God, for ever and ever.

See Lectionary for Mass, *nos. 784-788.*

PRAYER OVER THE GIFTS

Pray, brethren . . .

Lord,
receive the gifts and prayers which we offer to you
as we celebrate the beginning of this religious profession.
Grant that these first fruits of your servants
may be nourished by your grace
and be the promise of a richer harvest.

We ask this through Christ our Lord.

> *Preface of Religious Profession, page 132; intercessions of the*
> *eucharistic prayers, pages 125-127.*

Communion Rite

Whoever does the will of God is my
brother, my sister, and my mother
(Mark 3:35).

PRAYER AFTER COMMUNION

Let us pray.

> *Pause for silent prayer, if this has not preceded.*

Lord,
may the sacred mysteries we have shared bring us joy.
By their power grant that your servants
may constantly fulfill the religious duties they now take up
and freely give their service to you.

We ask this through Christ our Lord.

2. PERPETUAL PROFESSION

A

Introductory Rites

I rejoiced when I heard them say: let
us go to the house of the Lord.
Jerusalem, we stand as pilgrims in
your court! (Psalm 122:1-2)

OPENING PRAYER

God our Father,
you have caused the grace of baptism
to bear such fruit in your servants
that they now strive to follow your Son more closely.
Let them rightly aim at true evangelical perfection
and increase the holiness and apostolic zeal of your Church.

We ask this through our Lord Jesus Christ, your Son,
who lives and reigns with you and the Holy Spirit,
one God, for ever and ever.

See Lectionary for Mass, *nos. 784-788.*

PRAYER OVER THE GIFTS

Pray, Brethren . . .

Lord,
accept the gifts and the vows of your servants.
Strengthen them by your love
as they profess the evangelical counsels.

We ask this through Christ our Lord.

Preface of Religious Profession, page 132.

*In the eucharistic prayers, the offering of the professed may be
mentioned according to the texts below:*

I. FOR MEN

a) *In Eucharistic Prayer I, the special form of* Father, accept
this offering *is said:*

Father, accept and sanctify this offering
from your whole family and from these your servants
which we make to you on the day of their profession.
By your grace
they have dedicated their lives to you today.

When your Son returns in glory,
may they share in the joy of unending paschal feast.

[Through Christ our Lord. Amen.]

b) *In the intercessions of Eucharistic Prayer II, after the words* and all the clergy, *there is added:*

Lord, remember also these our brothers
who have today dedicated themselves to serve you always.
Grant that they may always raise their minds and hearts to you
and glorify your name.

c) *In the intercessions of Eucharistic Prayer III, after the words* your Son has gained for you, *there is added:*

Strengthen also these servants of yours in their holy purpose,
for they have dedicated themselves
by the bonds of religious consecration to serve you always.
Grant that they may give witness in your Church
to the new and eternal life won by Christ's redemption.

d) *In the intercessions of Eucharistic Prayer IV, the professed may be mentioned in this way:*

. . . bishop, and bishops and clergy everywhere.
Remember these our brothers
who unite themselves more closely to you today
by their perpetual profession.
Remember those who take part in this offering . . .

II. FOR WOMEN

a) *In Eucharistic Prayer I, the special form of* Father, accept this offering *is said:*

Father, accept and sanctify this offering
from your whole family and from these your servants
which we make to you on the day of their consecration.
By your grace
they join themselves more closely to your Son today.
When he comes in glory at the end of time,
may they joyfully meet him.

[Through Christ our Lord. Amen.]

b) *In the intercessions of Eucharistic Prayer II, after the words*
and all the clergy, *there is added:*

Remember all these sisters of ours
who have left all things for your sake
so that they might find you in all things
and by forgetting self serve the needs of all.

c) *In the intercessions of Eucharistic Prayer III, after the words*
your Son has gained for you, *there is added:*

Lord, strengthen these servants of yours in their holy purpose
as they strive to follow Christ your Son in consecrated holiness
by giving witness to his love in their religious life.

d) *In the intercessions of Eucharistic Prayer IV, the professed
may be mentioned in this way:*

. . . bishop, and bishops and clergy everywhere.
Remember our sisters who have consecrated themselves
    to you today
by the bond of religious profession.
Remember those who take part in this offering . . .

Communion Rite   *I am nailed with Christ to the
cross; I am alive, not by my own
life but by Christ's life within me
(Galatians 2:19-20).*

PRAYER AFTER COMMUNION

Let us pray.

Pause for silent prayer, if this has not preceded.

Lord,
as we share these sacred mysteries,
we pray for these your servants
who are bound to you by their holy offering.
Increase in them the fire of your Holy Spirit
and unite them in eternal fellowship with your Son,
who is Lord for ever and ever.

SOLEMN BLESSING

May God who is the source of all good intentions
enlighten your minds and strengthen your hearts.
May he help you to fulfill with steadfast faith all
    you have promised.
R. Amen.

May the Lord enable you to travel in the joy of Christ
as you follow along his way,
and may you gladly share each other's burdens.
R. Amen.

May the love of God unite you and make you a true family,
praising his name and showing forth Christ's love.
R. Amen.

May almighty God,
the Father, and the Son, + and the Holy Spirit,
bless all of you who have taken part in these sacred celebrations.
R. Amen.

B

I will offer sacrifice in your temple; I will fulfill the vows my lips have promised (Psalm 66:13-14).

OPENING PRAYER

Lord, holy Father,
confirm the resolve of your servants (N. and N.).
Grant that the grace of baptism,
which they wish to strengthen with new bonds,
may work its full effect in them,
so that they may offer you their praise
and spread Christ's kingdom with apostolic zeal.

We ask this through our Lord Jesus Christ, your Son,
who lives and reigns with you and the Holy Spirit,
one God, for ever and ever.

See Lectionary for Mass, *nos. 784-788.*

PRAYER OVER THE GIFTS

Pray, brethren . . .

Lord,
accept the offerings of your servants
and make them a sign of salvation.
Fill with the gifts of your Holy Spirit
those whom you have called by your fatherly providence
to follow your Son more closely.

We ask this through Christ our Lord.

Preface of Religious Profession, page 132; intercessions of the eucharistic prayers, as in the preceding Mass.

Communion Rite

Taste and see the goodness of the Lord; blessed is he who hopes in God (Psalm 34:9).

PRAYER AFTER COMMUNION

Let us pray.

Pause for silent prayer, if this has not preceded.

Lord,
may the reception of this sacrament
and the solemnizing of this profession bring us joy.
Let this twofold act of devotion
help your servants to serve the Church and humankind
in the spirit of your love.

We ask this through Christ our Lord.

SOLEMN BLESSING

God inspires all holy desires and brings them to fulfillment.
May he protect you always by his grace
so that you may fulfill the duties of your vocation
with a faithful heart.
R. Amen.

May he make each of you a witness
and sign of his love for all people.
R. Amen.

May he make those bonds
with which he has bound you to Christ on earth
endure for ever in heavenly love.
R. Amen.

May almighty God,
the Father, and the Son, + and the Holy Spirit,
bless all of you who have taken part in this celebration.
R. Amen.

3. RENEWAL OF VOWS

*The entrance and communion antiphons, if used, may be taken
from one of the three preceding Masses.*

OPENING PRAYER

God our Father,
guide of humankind and ruler of creation,
look upon these your servants
who wish to confirm their offering of themselves to you.
As the years pass by,
help them to enter more deeply into the mystery of the Church
and to dedicate themselves more generously
to the good of humankind.

We ask this through our Lord Jesus Christ, your Son,
who lives and reigns with you and the Holy Spirit,
one God, for ever and ever.

See Lectionary for Mass, *nos. 784-788.*

PRAYER OVER THE GIFTS

Pray, brethren . . .

Lord,
look mercifully upon the gifts of your people
and upon the renewed offering by our brothers (sisters)
of their chastity, poverty, and obedience.
Change these temporal gifts into a sign of eternal life
and conform the minds of those who offer them
to the likeness of your Son
who is Lord for ever and ever.

*Preface of Religious Profession, page 132; intercessions of the
eucharistic prayers, as in the preceding Masses.*

PRAYER AFTER COMMUNION

Let us pray.

Pause for silent prayer, if this has not preceded.

Lord,
now that we have received these heavenly sacraments,
we pray that your servants will trust only in your grace,
be strengthened by the power of Christ
and be protected with the help of the Holy Spirit.

We ask this through Christ our Lord.

PREFACE OF RELIGIOUS PROFESSION

Priest: The Lord be with you.

People: And also with you.

Priest: Lift up your hearts.

People: We lift them up to the Lord.

Priest: Let us give thanks to the Lord our God.

People: It is right to give him thanks.

Father, all-powerful and ever-living God,
we do well always and everywhere to give you thanks
through Jesus Christ our Lord.

He came, the Son of a Virgin Mother,
named those blessed who were pure of heart,
and taught by his whole life the perfection of chastity.

He chose always to fulfill your holy will
and became obedient even to dying for us,
offering himself to you as a perfect oblation.

He consecrated more closely to your service
those who leave all things for your sake
and promised that they would find a heavenly treasure.

And so, with all the angels and saints
we proclaim your glory
and join in their unending hymn of praise:

Holy, holy, holy Lord, God of power and might,
heaven and earth are full of your glory.
Hosanna in the highest.
Blessed is he who comes in the name of the Lord.
Hosanna in the highest.

III. TWENTY-FIFTH OR FIFTIETH ANNIVERSARY OF RELIGIOUS PROFESSION

This Mass may be celebrated, using white vestments, on all days except the Sundays of Advent, Lent and Easter, solemnities, Ash Wednesday and the weekdays of Holy Week. The entrance and communion antiphons may be taken from one of the preceding Masses.

OPENING PRAYER

God of faithfulness,
enable us to give you thanks
for your goodness to N., our brother/sister.
Today he/she comes to rededicate that gift
which he/she first received from you.
Intensify within him/her your spirit of perfect love,
that he/she may devote himself/herself more fervently
to the service of your glory
and the work of salvation.

We ask this through our Lord Jesus Christ, your Son,
who lives and reigns with you and the Holy Spirit,
one God, for ever and ever.

PRAYER OVER THE GIFTS

Pray, brethren . . .

All-powerful God,
together with these gifts
accept the offering of self
which N., our brother/sister, wishes to reaffirm today.

By the power of your Spirit
conform him/her more truly
to the likeness of your beloved Son.

We ask this through Christ our Lord.

Preface of Religious Profession, page 132.

PRAYER AFTER COMMUNION

Let us pray.

Pause for silent prayer, if this has not preceded.

God of love,
in this joyful anniversary celebration
you have fed us
with the body and blood of your Son.
Refreshed by heavenly food and drink
may our brother/sister, N., advance happily on that journey
which began in you and leads to you.

Grant this through Christ our Lord.